"I've been waiting for sor
Finally, a step by step guide for small businesses and non-profits to acquire corporate sponsorship dollars. Brilliant! On behalf of event planners everywhere, thank you, thank you, thank you!"

— Shelly Rice, Founder
Chocolate Blues and Business

"The days of a donor 'signing the check' just to get your organization off their back are over. The donor is looking for a win, too! *Relationships Raise Money* will help every organization who is seeking sponsorship to develop lasting relationships with their donors, resulting in long-term viable organizations."

— Leslie Knight, Founder
Knight Performance Management
Author, *Powerful Women: They're Not Men in Drag*

"Roberto Candelaria is one of the most genuine, gifted and caring people I have ever had the pleasure of working with, and his extensive knowledge and understanding of both corporate sponsorships, the non-profit world as well as for profit are only exceeded by his generosity and service to others."

— Patty Farmer, Winner
Best Business Connector in Dallas (2010)
Author, *Make Your Connections Count*

"Hands on, straight forward, and direct. If you follow his plan, success is inevitable."

— Angela Mitchell Hudson, Founder
HOPE SPS2

"As festival designers, we are always looking to develop new relationships with local and regional sponsors. The guidance within Roberto's book provides us with the tools to strengthen our existing sponsor programs and to develop new, professional relationships with corporate sponsors."

— Kathi Danielson, President
Performance & Event Management, LLC

"Your mind works in beautiful patterns and sees amazing possibilities, Roberto Candelaria! Thanks for being who you are and sharing your talents with the world."

— Sheryl Sitts, Founder and CIO
Journey of Possibilities

"Roberto is a positive self initiative business partner, consistently thinking of how to improve services and customer relations. It's always a pleasure dealing with Roberto."

— Elena Guajardo, Former Councilwoman
City of San Antonio

"This is great for you and all the charities who will be able to do more good in the world because you believed in this book and your purpose in the grand tapestry of life."

— Melissa Vrazel-Ramirez, Founder
Gentle Blessings

"Roberto was a key liaison in our partnerships. He helped bridge our organizations and promoted both companies to the community. His ability to network with the community proved essential to our marketing initiatives and helped us develop our own relationships within the community."

— Chase Martin, Managing Principal
Planet Chase, LLC

"Roberto Candelaria is a wealth of knowledge and one of the most creative thinkers I know. He has extensive experience working with non-profits. I am new to the non-profit world, have never been involved with fundraising and had no idea where to start. His book and expertise makes it doable and non-threatening. I appreciate the structured approach and guidance he offers along with his willingness to take self-less action to make connections and business happen. Roberto combines his heart and expertise in business making him a top notch speaker, coach and professional in this field."

— Suzanne Jarvis, Executive Director
Living Forward Alliance

"Looking for an MBA level education on how to secure corporate sponsorships? Stop reading, and go buy this book. Right now! You've just been admitted to sponsorship university."

— Jeremiah Trnka, Founder
Rebuild America Challenge

RELATIONSHIPS
RAISE
MONEY

A GUIDE TO CORPORATE SPONSORSHIP

Tonbeer

Always follow your dreams
& love your life!

RELATIONSHIPS
RAISE
MONEY

A GUIDE TO CORPORATE SPONSORSHIP

ROBERTO C. CANDELARIA
AUTHOR/SPEAKER/COACH

FOREWORD BY:
BARRY SPILCHUK, COAUTHOR
A CUP OF CHICKEN SOUP FOR THE SOUL

RELATIONSHIPSRAISEMONEY.COM
SPONSORSHIPBOOTCAMP.COM

Relationships Raise Money:
A Guide to Corporate Sponsorship

Copyright 2011 by Roberto C. Candelaria

PUBLISHED BY:
Calidad Marketing, LLC
PO Box 40854
Houston, TX 77240-0854
877-991-9925

ISBN: 978-0-9847555-0-9

For information regarding special discounts for bulk purchases, please contact Calidad Marketing, LLC or the author at 877-991-9925 or Info@HumanReturns.com.

Published in Houston, Texas by Calidad Marketing, LLC.

FIRST PUBLISHED: 2011

AUTHOR PHOTO BY: Marsha Anderson

INTERIOR LAYOUT BY: Jeremiah Trnka (jeremiah@jeremiahtrnka.com)

This book is dedicated to all the volunteers who give back to worthy causes. Thank you for making a difference! May this book serve as a road map to success in securing corporate sponsorships.

"Follow your passions, believe in karma, and you won't have to chase your dreams, they will come to you."

— Randy Pausch

Earnings Disclaimer & Forward Looking Statements

When addressing any financial matters in this book, Calidad Marketing, LLC, Human Returns and Roberto Candelaria have made every effort to accurately represent our products and programs and their ability to grow your business. The representation of the potential of our products and programs is subject to our interpretation.

While the earnings potential for those that use our products and programs is usually very encouraging, you acknowledge that your earning potential is subject to many different factors. We value hard work and dedication, and you realize those are two of the many different factors that determine your individual success. We do not believe in any "get rich schemes" and believe that you are responsible for your own actions, results, and successes.

We make no warranty or guarantee of any kind that you will experience any level of earnings by using our products and programs. Any examples we have provided should not be interpreted as any guarantee of earnings. Any products and programs that we offer should not be mistaken for "Get Rich Schemes."

We are not Attorneys or CPA's and we cannot and do not offer you any direct financial advice, nor are we responsible for any financial decisions you make. You alone are responsible for your actions, results and success in life. It should be clear to you that we do not make any warranties or guarantees that you will achieve any results for the information presented in this product and program. It should also be clear that we offer no professional legal, medical, psychological or financial advice. It is your decision and responsibility to discuss the legality and financial soundness of any decision you make with a qualified professional before you make such decision.

This program may include "forward-looking statements." Forward-looking statements include information concerning future results. Words such as "believes," "expects," "anticipates," "intends," "plans," "estimates," "projects," "forecasts," and future or conditional verbs such as "will," "may," "could," "should," and "would" as well as any other statement that necessarily depends on future events, are intended to identify forward-looking statements. Forward-looking statements are not guarantees, and they involve risks, uncertainties and assumptions. There can be no assurance that actual results will not differ materially from our expectations.

TABLE OF CONTENTS

You Want This Book If...

✓ You want to understand what can be sponsored.

✓ You want the secret to getting free media through your sponsors.

✓ You want to create effective sponsorship proposals that get results.

✓ You want to measure the effectiveness of your sponsorship campaigns.

✓ You want to persuade your sponsors to renew, year after year.

Acknowledgements

As we express our gratitude, we must never
forget that the highest appreciation is not to
utter words, but to live by them.

— John Fitzgerald Kennedy

Creating and writing this book has been an incredible experience, and there were a core group of people that supported and encouraged me as I dedicated a few months of my life to this book.

Leslie Knight, for her encouragement to develop this book, the coaching program and her never-ending dedication to the final project. I appreciate your feedback and thank you for helping me to re-clarify sections of this book. Thank you for your insights on drawing from the strengths of those around us and guiding me on how to best lead from my strengths. I am truly grateful to call you a mentor and friend. (LeslieKnight.com)

Rodolfo and Debbie Candelaria, my parents. Thank you for loving me and always allowing me to dream. I am eternally grateful for the example of love, dedication, and integrity that you both are.

Bonnie Karpay, for your constant guidance and support. You believed in me from day one, even when I had doubts about my ability. I am grateful for your friendship, support, and your never-ending work to connect Entrepreneurs with all of the resources they need to succeed.

Jeremiah Trnka, for everything you've done and continue to do! Thank you for your dedication to my success and helping me realize the full potential of my dreams, I am honored to call you my friend and a mentor.

Deborah Gilbert, for serving as a sounding board and supporter of my dreams! We really need to have a Route 44 Happy Hour.

Glenn Scott and James Reaser, for introducing me to the importance of giving back to my community and supporting great causes. You have been two of my biggest cheerleaders and mentors through the years, and I am grateful for your friendship and constant support.

Marisol C. Candelaria, my sister. You are an amazing educator, mother, and sister. Thank you for sharing your time and talents with me.

Berny Dohrmann, Founder of CEO Space. Thank you for creating an environment of cooperation and collaboration where entrepreneurs can find all of the resources they need to help make their dreams a reality. (CEOSpaceInternational.com)

Charles D. Sommerville, for your constant encouragement and friendship over the years. Thank you for always believing in me and for always being there.

Myrna Whitt, for never allowing me to give up and helping me past my fears. You are my angel and I am forever blessed because you are in my life.

Kim Burney, for your coaching, dedication, and guidance with this and other projects. Thank you for your commitment to help me spread this message to those that need it most.

Finally, Barry Spilchuk. Thank you for believing in me! The first time I heard you speak you said, "What is the cost of not doing what you say?" Remembering those words carried me through the completion of this book. Thank you does not express my gratitude for your willingness to write the foreword to this book. I cried the first time I read it, and still do to this day. A framed copy sits on my desk. When I'm having a rough day, I read your words and they remind me to keep on going. Thank you for living by your own advice!

Thank you to everyone else that has been a part of my life. I'm grateful for each one of you and the lessons I've learned from our time and experiences together.

FOREWORD

"If I agree to give $8.00 of every $20.00—*You're My Hero*®—book sale to the local Women's Shelter—how much will you give me back?"

"Barry, do you promise me the money will be going to the Women's Shelter?"

YES!

"Then I'll give you the whole $20.00 back!"

This was an actual conversation I had with the manager of a _____ store. Fill-in-the-blank. What kind of store? A *book* store?

NO.

Believe it or not…it was a *hardware store.* Canada's National Hardware / Home-care / Car-care store is Canadian Tire.

Why did I choose Canadian Tire to sell a book? Many reasons: In a book store, I would be competing against 40,000 other titles. At Canadian Tire, other than roadside maps and car manuals, I was the only book there! They had hundreds of people coming to the store everyday and on some days over a thousand people would frequent this ever-growing, community-minded local franchise.

The manager added, "I said 'YES' because I know you are going to bring people into my store!" He was right. In a space of 25 days we sold 1,900 books and donated over $17,000.00 to the Nipissing Women's Transition House. We also donated 750 books to the local Santa Claus Fund and another 1,600 books to our brave men and women in the Canadian Armed Forces. All this was made possible due to the generosity of our sponsor.

It was a Win-Win situation. As a matter of fact, *many* wins were attained and thousands of people benefitted because of two simple things:

1. I asked
2. Canadian Tire said *yes!*

At one point the store manager was standing there watching me autograph books for a line-up of people. He smiled at me, nodded and walked away saying, "I knew you would bring people into my store."

I share this real event to demonstrate to you the power of the book you have in your hands. Roberto Candelaria has written an amazing book that will assist you in evaluating, contacting and selling sponsors for your events and causes.

What you are holding in your hand at this very moment is a step-by-step guidebook to unravel the mystery of how Sponsorships work—AND—a manual that will give you the confidence to approach any sponsor with integrity and a Win-Win attitude.

Pay special attention to the 10-point Sponsorship Checklist, it will assist you in making a proposal that stacks the benefits for your Sponsor and will afford you a greater chance of getting a "YES" from your potential benefactor.

Another thing that is special about this book is the author himself. I have had the pleasure of working with Roberto when we were volunteering at a world class business seminar. I had the honor of teaching a class and I also had the pleasure and honor of working side-by-side with Roberto.

His ability to give and serve at high levels was for the sole purpose of ensuring that every student would have a magnificent experience over the eight-day event.

Roberto has infused that same selfless, giving attitude into the pages of this book for one reason—so you can read this book and enjoy your own personal journey of magnificence as you celebrate your life and your dreams to the highest level.

Happy reading!

— Barry Spilchuk

Founder, *You're My Hero®* Books

Coauthor, *A Cup of Chicken Soup for the Soul®*

Master Trainer, Canada's Public Speaking Academy

CanadasPublicSpeakingAcademy.com

INTRODUCTION

HUMAN RETURNS: THE POWER OF RELATIONSHIPS

I believe in the power of relationships. The effectiveness of your sponsorship campaign is a direct reflection of how well your organization understands this power. Your ability to partner with some of the numerous for-profit companies will often times determine the survival of your cause.

According to the National Center for Charitable Statistics (NCCS), there are over 1.5 million non-profit organizations operating in the United States[1] and there are many more for-profit companies. A large percentage of these organizations, both for-profit and non-profit, are not making full use of their existing relationships to secure sponsorship dollars to further their causes. Why? In my experience, I've found that either they either lack the resources to properly engage in an intelligent discussion about sponsorship or they fear their relationships are not strong enough to broach the subject.

> **SPONSORSHIP SECRET:** For-profit companies want to sponsor worthwhile causes! Knowledge and a little experience develop confidence and dispel F.E.A.R. (false expectations appearing real).

1 http://foundationcenter.org/getstarted/faqs/html/howmany.html

I was discussing the sponsorship process with a friend of mine who works for a major computer company to improve the chances of their approving proposals from my clients. Somewhere in the discussion she mentioned that in a previous year they hadn't spent their allocated sponsorship budget and so her budget was cut the next near. This intrigued me. While I know most companies have budgets, isn't it a good thing to come in under budget? In this case, NO! As a direct result of not awarding enough, basically all, of their sponsorship budget, their budget was cut the next year. Not only was the sponsorship budget cut, but her labor budget was also cut which meant she had to layoff some of her team.

Did you catch that? Jobs were lost because they didn't have enough projects that matched their values and their market. Would you like to be responsible for someone losing their job? I know I don't. Your contacts in the sponsorship world have a budget they need to exhaust every year. Why shouldn't some of those funds go to your organization or cause? If you don't ask, someone else will!

> **SPONSORSHIP SECRET:** The best way to help a prospective sponsor is to help them find a suitable home for the sponsorship dollars they must disperse every budget year.

Up over $5 Billion from 2008, global sponsorship spending continues an upward trend. How many other budgets do you know that are continuing to grow? Even in the current economy, companies are allocating more funds than ever towards sponsorship. Keep reading and learn how to get your piece of this multi-billion dollar pie!

Funding is available for your cause. In fact, IEG estimates approximately $48.7 Billion will be available for sponsorship in 2011 alone. The funding is there, all you need to do is learn how to ask.

WHERE DO I BEGIN?

Many years ago I had no idea where to begin when I first started securing sponsorships for the organizations for whom I volunteered. Not only was I unsure of where to start, I couldn't find the resources I desperately needed to become successful. This isn't unusual, as only an estimated 18% of non-profits have a department or staff dedicated to handling sponsorships for the organization and that percentage is even less in for-profit companies.

Over the past ten years I've had the honor of working with several organizations, for-profit and non-profit, and learned the sponsorship world from the ground up. It hasn't always been easy, and for the first few years, my proposals were rejected more often than they were accepted. Thankfully, one of the many things that my parents taught me was to never give up. My dad, who has had great success in sales, once told me that the only difference between us was that he had heard a lot more no's than I had.

I thought about that as I continued my journey in the sponsorship world and one day an idea came to my mind. What if I could engage the sponsorship department that had just rejected my proposal in a conversation, instead of merely hearing "No" and walking away? I did this, and much to my surprise, the young lady I was working with gave me the top 3 reasons my proposal wasn't approved and she told me how to increase my opportunity for approval the next time. I was blown away! I really didn't think they'd lay out the road map to being successfully funded by their company.

Just to make sure this wasn't an isolated incident, I had the same conversation with a different company that had not funded another proposal, and received a similar response. I realized I was onto something and started calling just about every company that hadn't funded one of our proposals. I spoke with administrative assistants, sponsorship coordinators, and even a few VPs of Marketing throughout the US. Through these conversations I developed a road map that resulted in the approval of a greater percentage of my proposals.

These experiences reminded me of one of the most important lessons my parents taught me, the importance of relationships. When it came to securing sponsors for one-time, annual, or virtual events, it came down to the quality of my relationship with the sponsor, every time. Over time, I learned five keys to improve the quality of my sponsorship relationships:

FIRST: Relationships take time. Think of the people and businesses with which you have a relationship. Did you start out as instant friends? Of course not, it takes time to get to know people and to build their trust. Developing sponsors to support your organization is not like selling encyclopedias door-to-door. Your organization is going to be around for a long time, so be patient and invest time in building a good relationship with the people and organizations that will come to share the passion and mission of your non-profit.

SECOND: Be supportive of the prospect. Be willing to meet for coffee to discuss your project and to provide any information and backup data the prospect may request. If he asks for time to consider your project, don't push for the close. You are not selling an appliance or a used car. It is very common for more than one party, or even a board, to be part of the decision making process. Be willing to make more than one visit and to be asked to speak to more than one party. You are the matchmaker, looking for those great connections, and that doesn't happen instantaneously.

THIRD: Be respectful of the prospect's time. He may not have a lot of time for coffee meetings. If he tells you he has 15 minutes, prepare a 10-minute presentation. This way at the end of your presentation, he has time to ask questions. Don't assume that once he hears about the great work your organization does he will be more than happy to cancel all meetings and spend the afternoon with you. If you are calling a business, the person you are talking to is on the time clock and has other commitments. Present your case well, meaning concisely, and be ready to leave.

Fourth: Be respectful of the prospect's timetable. If you are a procrastinator, then it is definitely time to change. It never works to rush a sponsor. If you are working on a large event, like a golf tournament or musical festival, the effort should begin several months to a year in advance. Even smaller events require a great deal of planning. There is an old saying in business, "A lack of planning on your end does not constitute an emergency on mine." This is very true in the sponsorship world.

Fifth: Conduct your affairs in a professional, business-like manner. This demonstrates both organizational stability and your consideration for the prospective sponsor. You might be smaller, but your conduct can sway their opinion in your favor.

Because of the relationships I've developed, the teams I've led & served with secured sponsorships from well-known brands such as BMW, DELL Computers, Southwest Airlines and State Farm Insurance—just to name a few. You see, relationships raise money. Basically you must like each other; have a mutual respect for and understanding of each other. You must feel good when you work together. That is what makes a quality relationship. That is true affinity.

Your company, organization, or cause need not fear that they lack anything substantial to offer a potential sponsor, such as free tickets or a logo on a shirt or website. Corporate sponsors aren't really involved for the free tickets to whatever event you give them. These corporations are sponsoring your organization or cause because your clients are part of their target market. These companies are looking for valuable introductions and to gain exposure to new clients in their target market through your event.

Are you hearing me? You have something the sponsor wants, access and introductions to new relationships you create. The sponsor has something you need, access to resources, including funding. All you need to do is create a mutually beneficial relationship with the sponsor to access his resources.

In this book, I'll not only give you the information you need to create profitable sponsorship campaigns, I'll show you how to utilize your organization's existing relationships to develop sponsors.

This book will help you understand:

- The definitions of sponsorship
- What can be sponsored
- How to create sponsorship campaigns that get results
- Your proposal: Opportunity or Investment?

- How to measure the effectiveness of your sponsorship campaign
- How to get your sponsors to renew (My favorite part!)

I'll do my part to help you succeed. I cannot stress enough the importance of pausing to complete the exercises as you read. I'm showing you a well-paved road. All you have to do is consciously and carefully drive down the road!

Let's begin!

Of all the things I've done, the most vital is coordinating those who work with me and aiming their efforts at a certain goal.

— WALT DISNEY

CHAPTER 1

THE BIG PICTURE

Are you a newly credentialed 501(c)(3) or an established organization making their first foray into the world of sponsorships?

Maybe you're a for-profit company looking into sponsorship for the first time.

The two most common questions I am asked by organizations in these stages are:

1. Why would someone sponsor me?
2. Do I really need big name sponsors?

The answer to the first question is simple: Sponsorships are a mutually beneficial business transaction. You want support and credibility. They want access to your customers. You want a speaking platform. They want a copy of the night's email list. You want something from them and they gain something from you in return.

The answer to the second question is "YES!" Sponsorships, more than anything, are an important catalyst and can lend more credibility to your organization than you could ever hope to buy. Their logo alone on any of your promotional materials or websites will cause some people to pause and take another look at you, and cause many more to take action of some kind in your favor. People respect and respond to the familiar. They are hardwired that way, and someday when you are the big cheese in the industry, you too will rely on that behavior.

For now, you will have to make do with "borrowing" credibility from familiar brands as in the following example. Imagine you are a hiring manager for a small business and you have two very qualified candidates applying for the position of "marketing director" for your company.

Applicant A has a B.S. in Marketing, from a good school, and 4 years of experience with some small, but not well known, companies. Applicant B has the same amount of education and experience, but his work history carries the experience of working with a Fortune 500 company and references from his supervisors. Who would you hire?

Most would hire Applicant B because of the name recognition that comes with a Fortune 500 company. The internal dialogue goes something like "Well, I'm sure with 4 years' experience with a Fortune 500 company, this guy knows his stuff."

In reality, Applicant A, whom we have almost completely forgotten by now, could have been a better fit job for you. He might even have worked harder just to prove himself. Applicant B may have lucked into his position and was quickly "downsized." But alas, we shall never know, because 99% of the world will choose Applicant B.

Don't dismay over this! Understand it so that you can make it work for you when the time is right. Now tell me how important does being sponsored by someone as well known as a Fortune 500 company sound to you? Would you still be excited if they only gave you a few hundred dollars and the use of their logo? You should be!

What I'm trying to drill into your head is the power of a brand name and how powerful gaining just the use of their name can be. Go for the BIG ONES if you think you are ready. Go for the largest brands that have a local rep in your area, but NEVER go unprepared. People are still people and first impressions are EVERYTHING.

Another powerful thing a logo does is attract more logos, and by that I mean sponsors. Think about it like 3 children playing with toys. No one wants the new toy until one of the children picks it up and begins to play with it. Suddenly ALL the children want that specific toy! This happens with sponsors too and it will work for you. Get a major sponsor to let you use their logo and the others will practically jump on board. It's the first one that's the hardest.

Once you have thrown a sponsored event, you can continue to use the power of their logos to your advantage, even if they do not sponsor you the second time around. How? You can list them as previous sponsors when you solicit a new sponsorship! "Last year we had Red Bull, Intel and Napa Auto sponsor our event" goes over a lot better than being hosted by "what's his name?"

I'm not saying that smaller, homegrown sponsors don't have their place in all this either. Small sponsors are a great asset, especially when you are trying to get the support of your local community. They are not to be overlooked in favor of the larger sponsors. They are merely different and offer different perks

A CRASH COURSE

Here is where I try to grab your attention and hold it just long enough to convey the bare essentials. Imagine you are hovering far above the earth, looking down for a specific home address—kind of like Google Earth. We will keep zooming in until we find the house we are looking for, so here we go. Big picture time!

To understand a sponsor is to understand what they want from you. Understanding what you can give them will help you know how to approach them. What do they want and how will they measure your ability to give them what they want? I know from experience they will want to know about your audience. So if you don't have one you'd better start building one now. The more people you have, the more power you have. Period.

Building an audience means nothing more than creating some kind of event and getting people to actually show up. That's right. You need to learn how to get bodies through the door or on your mailing lists. It's not that hard, but it's not simple either. I personally believe the best way to practice is through an event or activity.

An event or activity usually consists of:

- A venue (a place to gather)
- Entertainment
- Refreshments
- You, a great host and conversationalist
- A memento for your guests to take home with them as well, even if it is nothing more than the night's program.

Especially in the non-profit world, you should plan and execute some type of event to build a following and a track record and to show that it will be a recurring event. In the for-profit world, we show our demographic reach by collecting data about the buying trends of our target markets. For profit and non-profit companies, the key is to prove that you have a following and that your following shares some of the same core values as your potential sponsor.

If you already have an attendance record, great! That will be your ticket to getting your foot in the door with the target sponsor. Now he or she will want to know your audience demographics: average age, sex, income, race, you name it. They want to determine if your audience is a good fit for their product or service or the company values they represent. If you tend to attract 50 year old, middle class housewives, a brewery is probably not the best sponsorship match for your demographic. Got it? Good.

The sponsor will also want to know how you are promoting the event. Having past examples of articles, press releases, flyers and ad campaigns are a sure fire way to grab their attention. I'll list many of the areas in media, internet, and retail that you can use to promote your event in later chapters.

Keep your sponsor in the loop during the entire process, from the time they sign the agreement through the closing of the event. You don't want to overwhelm them with too much information though, so choose your contact carefully and wisely.

You will also need a process for gathering feedback from the sponsor, the attendees and vendors. Did you meet everyone's expectations? Were all commitments fulfilled? Are your sponsors and guests happy? What did people think? Keep the feedback loop alive by posting free, downloadable pictures of the event on your website or posting articles about your sponsors. It drives traffic while giving back to the community and your sponsors.

Lastly, don't forget to thank people. Take the time to express your gratitude to the sponsors, vendors and even your attendees.

Once you have completed the cycle, you are ready to begin again. Your next event will be bigger and better since you're now armed with the knowledge and confidence to succeed!

Now that you've seen the big picture, let's drill down into the details of sponsorship.

*People don't know what they want until
you show it to them.*

— STEVE JOBS

CHAPTER 2

WHAT EXACTLY IS A SPONSORSHIP?

As I speak with groups around the country, I have found a common misconception surrounding the idea of sponsorship: any free item given to your organization or cause qualifies as sponsorship. This is not the case.

Most contributions to non-profit organizations fall into two main categories, donations and sponsorship. We'll discuss the difference in greater detail later. Sponsorship has evolved over the years and, in many ways, continues to evolve as one of the most important parts of a company's marketing budget. When executed properly, sponsorship dollars generate a larger ROI than most forms of traditional advertising. Traditional media still has its place in advertising, but we are seeing more companies shift a larger portion of their advertising budgets to sponsorship. Unlike traditional advertising, sponsorship allows a company to stay front of mind with their target market by tying an emotion to the positive experience of an event you create. The goodwill created is priceless.

For the purpose of this book, we'll use the definition of Sponsorship from IEG.

SPONSORSHIP: "A cash and/or in-kind fee paid to a property (typically in sports, arts, entertainment or causes) in return for access to the exploitable commercial potential associated with that property." [1]

In other words, companies are paying for the opportunity to market to their target demographic through your organization. They want to pay you for access to your volunteers, board members, donors and clients.

As a side note, a "*property*" is the term most sponsorship divisions will use to describe your proposal. A property is the gala, event, entertainment or other cause for which they are considering partnering with your organization.

Sponsorship is a business relationship and, like all relationships, takes time to develop correctly and well. Someone simply giving your organization a gift certificate or free food is NOT a sponsorship. This would be considered a donation and we'll touch more on the differences between them later.

Here's a brief, 10-point snapshot into the head of a sponsor. Familiarize yourself with these questions. Taking a critical look at your business, using the outline below, can show you some early weak spots where you need to *tidy up*.

---

1 http://www.sponsorship.com/IEG-Forum.aspx?forumid=1&threadid=5153

The 10 Point Sponsor Value Checklist

In corporate America, most companies you approach will have a set of guidelines to determine if your event or opportunity qualifies as a good use of their funds. Some of the things they consider are:

1. Does the sponsorship match our values and the market we are trying to reach?
2. Will this gain us exposure to new customers within our target market?
3. How much media exposure will we receive and how does that compare to our media buys?
4. Is there a possibility for a multi-year agreement?
5. What comps (value added items) are we given for making your dream happen?
6. Who are some of the previous sponsors?
7. Would a competitor sponsor the event should we decline?
8. What is the track record of success for this organization?
9. What media exposure will there be?
10. Are there any celebrities or politicians affiliated with the event?

As you consider these questions you may get new ideas that you need to implement into your promotion plan and event planning to attract quality attendees. These are all thoughts that will make you $$$ and you are right to pause and adjust your plan, and hopefully your perception too!

WHAT CAN BE SPONSORED?

This is one of my favorite questions and one that is often asked by people unfamiliar with securing sponsorships for their organization. Mel Stuart's movie *Willy Wonka & The Chocolate Factory* contains the best analogy to answer this question. Do you remember the movie? I hope you do, because it reminds me of the endless possibilities when it comes to sponsorships. In the scene I am thinking of, Willy Wonka guides the kids and parents to the chocolate factory and as he opens the vault door into paradise, the music starts and Willy Wonka speaks the words...

"Hold your breath. Make a wish. Count to three."

Then he sings...

"Come with me, and you'll be, in a world of pure imagination.."

It may seem a bit silly, but it paints an accurate picture. Do you remember that scene? That is the true power behind creating your sponsorship packages, imagination. Just as the varieties of candies, lollipops, and—of course—chocolate, offered inside Willy Wonka's chocolate factory were limitless, the possibilities for sponsorship are limitless too. As in years past, sponsorship just isn't for sport anymore. Sponsored properties (a term used by sponsors to refer to non-profit proposals) are limited by your imagination in devising them and your creativity in designing valuable packages for potential sponsors.

Here are examples of things you can have sponsored:

- Gala events
- Naming rights to the event or part of the event
- Exclusivity in any given category
- Bowling, golf, and other sports tournaments
- Your website
- Choice of venue
- Signage
- Hospitality suites
- Access to VIPs
- T-Shirts
- Vehicles for your organization
- Office/meeting space
- Media buys
- Seminars
- Promotion or sweepstakes
- Pre-sale ticket access
- Discounted tickets for their customers
- Coupon opportunities
- And much, much more…

TYPES OF SPONSORSHIPS

Many organizations wonder how to structure their sponsorships and what types of sponsorships to offer. While every successful sponsorship proposal contains a few key elements, it is up to you to decide what elements you need to make your campaign successful. Some of the most common forms of sponsorship include:

EVENT SPONSORSHIPS

- Title Sponsorships
- Activity Sponsorships
- Media Sponsorships

An event sponsorship allows companies you select to sponsor a major event that your organization hosts. Most events will have 2-4 main sponsorship levels available, with a handful of premium a la carte sponsorships also available. These events include Gala Dinners, Golf Tournaments, or any other major and/or annual event that your organization hosts.

Each event has two major goals: raise money and raise awareness. Small businesses and corporations will be interested in sponsoring your event for several reasons. A major motivation is the opportunity to gain access and exposure to your customers or donors. Your event provides them with an occasion to market their product and, as the scope of the event increases, the opportunity for more exposure through the various media outlets (TV, radio, print, social media).

Possibly one of the most appealing aspects of sponsoring a large event is media coverage. If the event is large enough to be covered by a local or national media source, sponsors will be very interested in the additional exposure. Another reason that companies sponsor is simply to show that they are a part of, and support, their local community. Event sponsorship provides a way for executives to interact with their community and the media.

> **SPONSORSHIP SECRET:** Attend local, state, or national charity events to meet the executives that handle sponsorships for major companies? Key executives, and their PR teams like keeping themselves in the media through attendance at high profile charity events.

A TITLE SPONSORSHIP: Names an event, or building— whatever the case may be—after the main sponsor such as the PGA Tour's FedEx Cup. Perhaps you work for an organization that works with at-risk youth, and you want to build a facility that has basketball courts and other athletic accommodations not generally available to the youth in that particular neighborhood. Something you can offer sponsors is the opportunity to have that building named after their company. Perhaps you're hosting a run/walk to raise money for your organization. You can name the event after your sponsor. This is a great way for companies to get publicity and can be a very successful tool for gaining sponsorship.

ACTIVITY SPONSORSHIP: Differs from event sponsorship in several ways and can be viewed as different types of sponsorships. An activity, unlike an event, is normally a smaller affair that is usually meant to target the group with which your organization is concerned. Rather than being a huge fundraiser, an activity is a way to reach out to the community.

For example, your organization might plan a fair in the park with small attractions, activities and concessions. The main purpose of this activity is to connect with people and give back to the community. Your main sponsorship request in this instance would be to cover the cost of the event.

Another example of activity sponsorship would be raising money for a group of children to take a field trip to a zoo or museum. It is always important to explain in your proposal, the purpose of your activity and the expected impact it will have on the group or community in your proposal.

Another type of activity sponsorship is one that deals with a specific activity within a larger event. Examples of activity sponsorships include lunches, parties, and networking events.

MEDIA SPONSORSHIPS: An excellent way for your organization to gain recognition. One way to get media sponsorship is to find a program with a similar outreach.

For instance, perhaps your organization raises money to assist low-income families to acquire healthcare. A news program with an outreach offering free vaccines for children in low-income communities might be interested in partnering with you in an event.

DONATIONS VS. SPONSORSHIPS

How are sponsorships and donations different? Merriam-Webster defines a donation as, "the making of a gift especially to a charity or public institution." [1] Donations are basically free money, free product, free advertising and just about anything else that is given to your organization with no strings attached. Your donors aren't looking for anything in return, whereas with sponsorship, your organization is responsible for specific deliverables.

Donations are a very important aspect of fundraising, and it is important to note that, while the company may not be receiving any commercial gain through the non-profit organization, the donors still benefit. Donations are tax deductible, so even those donating can profit from the exchange.

While donations are a vital part of the process, sponsorships offer the opportunity for more substantial and long term funding and should be a major focus of the non-profit staff. Sponsorships, unlike donations, are

---

1 http://www.merriam-webster.com/dictionary/donation

a reciprocal relationship in which both the benefactor and the recipient reap material profit.

For example, a company might financially sponsor an event or project and, in return, that non-profit organization advertises that company's product at the event. The main difference between donations and sponsorship is that with donations, the non-profit has no obligations to fulfill while in sponsorship, both parties look to profit from the exchange.

Some measurable returns, which you can provide a sponsor, include:

- Event signage
- Media coverage: web, print, radio, and television advertising
- Access to the mailing list for the specific event
- Opportunity for a giveaway

Let's look at all these options in a little more detail.

Event Signage

Have you ever been to an event that had signs advertising different companies placed throughout the building? Those signs are sponsor advertising. This is common in sporting events as well as most National and televised events. These events place signs around the area so that everyone in the audience can view them. This tactic can be incorporated into practically any type of event, including your website.

Perhaps the event is a 5K run/walk to raise money for a local non-profit organization. An easy way to advertise for donors would be to place signs around the running track. This can be further expanded. Those companies, which provide the most funding, can have their advertisements placed on banners at the starting point and the finish line. These spots are photographed the most and will likely be included in a local newspaper. Because of this placement they can be presented to prospective sponsors as prime locations. Sponsors will always find your pitch more appealing if they know that you have some form of media coverage, which can expand the reach of their advertisements.

MEDIA COVERAGE

There are several forms of media coverage. The first, and perhaps the easiest one to acquire, is web or Internet advertising. As society moves forward, and technology gains an increasingly prominent place in the world, web advertising is becoming an integral part of sponsor advertising. Many of you probably have a Twitter or Facebook page. If you do, then you have seen media advertisement. In fact, you can even create a page for your organization and purchase targeted advertising through one or both of these venues.

Your organization's website is another very important advertising tool. You can dedicate a section of your website to thanking your sponsors (use their logo) and promoting them with short articles. If you do not have a website for your organization one of your next priorities must be to make one. They are vital!

When presenting the possibilities for web advertising to your potential sponsor, include a quote of the "impressions" on your website. This simply refers to the number of times you website is viewed per hour, day, week or year. Sometimes, this information contains demographic data like region and software of the viewers of your website. Alexa (www.alexa. com) and Google Analytics are common sources for this information. Your site developer will be able to help you.

Print advertising is a lower cost option of traditional media coverage. This includes newspapers, magazines and local newsletters. Many local communities and homeowner's associations circulate a newsletter that lists upcoming area events. This is a great way to publicize local non-profit events and is one of the easier sources of media advertising to obtain. Scout out any local newspapers and newsletters around the city in which the event is taking place and approach them about including an article covering your event. Don't overlook bulletin boards in local stores and restaurants. They are often happy to support community events.

The next level is the major newspapers. Most news-papers include a special section, in one of the midweek editions, devoted to news and events taking place in smaller geographic areas. While this is a harder, more competitive media outlet, it is an opportunity that should never be overlooked. Find intriguing ways to present your story that will catch the attention of your target media group. If you can include photos, the chances of your story being printed increase dramatically.

The next option is radio advertising. This is more difficult than the previously listed options, but is also more desirable. Many radio stations have a community announcement line on their websites from which they pick community organizations to announce on the air. These are often done on a first come, first serve basis. Furthermore, the radio program will be planned well in advance, so it is essential that you investigate this option early to get your organization near the top of the radio station's list.

Radio coverage appeals to potential sponsors since it informs a wider audience about the activity, the organization and the sponsors. Media coverage increases the number of people who hear about the event which, in turn, increases the number of people who attend the event. Sponsors are attracted to larger events because they offer more publicity and opportunity for their advertisements and products to be seen.

The final source is television advertising. While not everyone reads the newspaper or local newsletters, most people watch television, and even people that aren't big TV buffs will often watch the news. The best way to break into television advertising is to approach local news groups. This is more difficult since news programs have limited air time.

> **SPONSORSHIP SECRET:** Looking for a way to increase your visibility and chances to get media coverage? Consider asking a local celebrity (your weather man or other news celebrity) to emcee the event. Most of the time they are willing to do it, and it could possibly increase your chances of making the news!

Press releases are another option to get attention from local news stations. Often, news programs will do community recognition segments as a means of highlighting local heroes. Perhaps you could submit one of your organization's volunteers for this segment.

Human interest stories often receive news coverage and create an opportunity for your organization. If your organization has greatly assisted someone in the community who is willing to share their experience submit the story to the local news. (It is very important, however, that you first acquire the consent of the individual before submitting their story to the network. You do not want to offend anyone or receive bad press for having divulged personal information without consent.)

Another way to attract television coverage is by having a well-known keynote speaker, such as a famous athlete or other celebrity. Television is the hardest media to access but yields the greatest returns and is an avenue worth pursuing.

Access to Mailing Lists

Another way sponsors can benefit from your contributions is through access to the mailing list for the event. This way, the company can send a coupon or other item to the attendees as a means of promoting their product. This may not sound appealing, since no one wants to receive a large amount of spam mail or advertisements. The last thing you want to do is offend everyone on your mailing list.

Fortunately, you are not giving out the names and addresses of everyone on your mailing list. By sending an email on the sponsor's behalf you are acting as the conduit by which your members receive the specified item from the company. This protects everyone on your list and still allows sponsors to profit from your organization's network.

Opportunities for Giveaways

Everyone loves free stuff, right? You have likely seen promotional items such as pens, pencils, key chains, and water bottles with the company's name, website, and other information at events you have attended. These are often handed out for free as a means of advertisement. This is a great way for you to both acquire goods to pass out at an event, and to advertise your sponsors.

However, these examples of items/activities are not considered sponsorship. Your organization has not accepted an obligation to provide a measurable deliverable. You have not promised them something in return.

- Promotion or advertising your event
- Displays and/or booth space
- Scholarships
- Door prizes
- Event tickets, suites, etc.
- Hospitality suites
- Trips

Keep in mind that while these examples are not totally inclusive, there are no set rules as to what can or cannot be sponsored or donated. It is up to your organization to decide the difference between a donation and a sponsorship. This can, at times, be confusing because some of the items listed above may also be included as part of the benefits package that a sponsor offered. A set amount of your sponsorship dollars could be used to setup and offer a scholarship fund for example.

Hospitality suites at live events give your sponsors, key leadership and other VIPs an exclusive area that provides access to entertainment, food, beverage and sometimes gift bags. I often recommend that if your organization is having a larger event with a hospitality suite, that you sell the rights to the property. By doing so, you are essentially covering the cost of any associated expenses that were not covered by donations.

Always Be Mindful of Your Relationships

I can't say it enough times. When it comes to sponsorship, relationships are everything. Non-profits, as with many organizations, thrive off of their ability to create and maintain excellent rapport with their sponsors. The wider the networks of your organization are, the better your chances are to find individuals interested in investing in your organization. This does not only apply to donors and sponsors. The relationships within your organization are just as important. After all, no sponsor would be attracted to a group filled with dissension and internal strife.

Positive interactions are important to any organization and it is our job to nurture them. As an organization, there are many different levels of relationships that you are responsible for maintaining. Some of these relationships include your:

- Staff
- Board of Directors
- Volunteers
- Clients
- Donors
- Sponsors
- Vendors

Think about all of the relationships listed above. How does your organization measure up when it comes to cultivating and sustaining these relationships?

While there are other levels of relationships, these are the key relationships in any organization. If you take a closer look at the different levels of these interactions, you'll notice that every level is linked to every other level in one way or another. You'll also notice that most of these relationships share a common set of core values. We'll get more into core values later, as it relates to securing sponsors. For now, let's focus on addressing our core values and relationships, as it pertains to potential sponsorship opportunities.

To run a successful organization, you must view your interactions with people at all levels as a relationship to be properly maintained. An important aspect is trust. If the members of your organization do not trust each other, potential sponsors will not trust your organization. If your organization has developed a bad reputation in the community then it will be extremely difficult to find sponsors. This is why trust and fulfillment of promises are so vital.

If you offer a company a certain amount of advertisement or value in return for their sponsorship, be sure to deliver. Do things sometimes happen that prevent our follow through? YES! My suggestion, should that happen, is to visit with your sponsor and discuss the problem with the intention of working together to create a new plan for their sponsorship. By doing this you build trust and prove that they can count on you. Otherwise, there is no trust built or reliability perceived and the relationship will fall apart.

What happens when you tell your spouse, partner, or friend that you will do something and then you fail to do it? That person often loses confidence in you, and you must work to regain trust. Unlike a business relationship, however, your loved ones are more likely to give you a chance to redeem yourself. In a sponsorship relationship, it is practically impossible to regain the trust of the slighted party. So, when interacting with potential sponsors, it is essential that you act with integrity. View your interactions with that company as a special relationship and the offers you make to them as binding promises. Your success in finding great sponsors is ultimately dependent upon your success in building great relationships.

Is there ever a time to say "no" to a potential sponsor? I say yes, depending on the mission, vision, and purpose of your organization. Here are a few sponsorships that need to be considered on a case-by-case basis:

➤ Sponsorship by companies that produce or distribute alcoholic beverages. While this might be a fit for an event with an open bar, this would not be a fit for an organization whose purpose is supporting alcoholics in recovery.

➤ Any sponsorship that could cause public controversy or unwanted media attention. We should all strive to have our media attention focused on the work we do and the lives we change, not lack of judgment in securing suitable sponsors.

➢ Sponsorships from board members or key donors who could potentially benefit from a future vote or contract from the organization. These potentially represent a conflict of interest and should be considered on an individual basis.

➢ Sponsors that have not lived up to their previous commitments. Vet your sponsors. You know they are checking up on you.

Sponsorship isn't a difficult concept to grasp. Successful sponsorship starts with:

- An understanding of the sponsor's target market, values and needs
- Mutual trust and respect
- An imagination to create mutually beneficial sponsorship packages
- Anything else you would like to include

Before moving to the next chapter where we discuss planning:

1. Make a list of possible activities and events for which you would seek sponsors.

2. Make a list of organizations you would like to attract as sponsors.

3. Begin to address the questions in the Sponsor Value Checklist.

Picture yourself in your minds eye as having already achieved this goal. See yourself doing the things you'll be doing when you've reached your goal.

— EARL NIGHTINGALE

CHAPTER 3

Five Steps to Productive Sponsorships

The sponsorship process is very much like starting a new diet or exercise plan. Since most people have attempted to do one or both at some point in their life, I'll relate the sponsorship process to an exercise plan.

After several months out of the gym, I decided that it was time to go back. At first I tried to self-motivate, "come on, you know this is good for you." Yet without a plan and a solid foundation, I didn't make it very far. At times I drove to the gym, parked, and then decided I'd rather go back home than go inside to exercise.

I'm sure there are some people, who will laugh when they read this, but it's true and I've seen so many people do the same with diets as well. Did I change my mind because I didn't need to exercise? No. I allowed myself to change my mind because I hadn't prepared myself to achieve my objective, losing weight through exercise. The steps for a successful exercise program are the same steps for creating productive sponsorships:

1. Assess yourself
2. Set your goals
3. Research the options
4. Plan for success
5. Exercise

ASSESS YOURSELF

I recently visited my doctor for a hydrostatic body composition analysis. For this test they lowered me into a water therapy pool, I had to blow out all the air from my lungs, and then they weighed me. We repeated this process several times until the technician felt that she had an accurate reading and then went to enter the numbers in the computer. When she returned she asked if I had any expectations for the results. When I said no, she shared the results of the test with me.

It's one thing to know I need to lose weight or get back in shape, but it was another experience to have that analysis broken down for me. You see, that analysis was an accurate portrayal of where I was physically and helped me create and action plan to move forward and get results.

One of the hardest things for any organization or individual to do is to perform an honest self-assessment. Many of the organizations reading this book will need to take a deeper look at their core values and begin to find their own identity. Just as the body analysis provided me with factual feedback of where I was physically, your organization has to be ready to take a deep and honest look at what you stand for and identify areas that need to be improved to make yourself more attractive to sponsors. Before approaching any potential benefactors your organization must have a clearly defined purpose. These come mainly in the form of your mission, vision, and purpose statements.

In my fundraising program, *Cash for Your Cause: How to Raise Five Figures in 30 Days*, I outline a detailed plan to build effective case statements and resource development plans. To get you started, here are a few questions for you and your board or organizing committee to answer. If your organization is committee oriented, more than one person may be helping to answer the questions. A good practice is to have each person write down their answers, expectations and ideas independently. This will not only prevent the most persuasive and passionate individuals from swaying the group, but will require that everyone, at this level, have an intellectual connection and commitment to the organization's mission and vision.

One of the fastest ways to make your organization seem unstable is to have a mission or vision statement that's a moving target. Once again, make certain that all of the members of the Board are in sync. Remember those term papers you were forced to write in school? The teacher made you pick a topic, then narrow it down to a manageable size, and finally come up with a precise thesis statement. That is exactly the process used to complete this self-assessment. Hey, you really do get to use some of the things high school taught you in "real life." Hope you were paying attention!

1. Who are you? Who is the group of people who have joined together to form this organization, project, or event? What brought each of you together?

2. What does each member of the Board hope to accomplish through this organization?

3. Who do you wish to help? "The poor" or "everyone" is not sufficient. Which poor people, those in your community, the state, areas devastated by disasters, in a different country? Defining your target service market is essential.

4. What service or services do you intend to provide? Once you have decided on exactly who you want to help, you must outline what you want to do for them? (If you have decided to work with at-risk youth in a certain metropolitan area, how do you plan to accomplish this? Provide scholarships? Tutoring? After school and summer programs? It is possible that you would want to start out with limited services but leave option to expand open. Your mission statement can be broad enough to allow expansion of individual activities and services while providing a defined focus.)

5. What companies are already sponsoring organizations with similar values?

Once you have answered these questions, draft a mission statement, one which succinctly states who you serve, how you serve them, and why you serve them. Your mission statement should be narrow enough to define your target service recipients but at the same time allow the organization to grow. Try looking up some larger, well known non-profit's mission statements to get a better idea. Here are a few to get you started.

> **PETA:** "PETA focuses its attention on the four areas in which the largest numbers of animals suffer the most intensely for the longest periods of time: on factory farms, in the clothing trade, in laboratories, and in the entertainment industry. We also work on a variety of other issues, including the cruel killing of beavers, birds, and other 'pests' as well as cruelty to domesticated animals. PETA works through public education, cruelty investigations, research, animal rescue, legislation, special events, celebrity involvement, and protest campaigns."

> **AMNESTY INTERNATIONAL:** "Our vision is for every person to enjoy all the rights enshrined in the Universal Declaration of Human Rights and other international human rights standards. We are independent of any government, political ideology, economic

interest or religion and are funded mainly
by our membership and public donations."

THE AMERICAN RED CROSS, a humanitarian organization led by volunteers and guided by its
Congressional Charter and the Fundamental
Principles of the International Red Cross and
Red Crescent Movement, will provide relief
to victims of disaster and help people prevent,
prepare for, and respond to emergencies.

Before proceeding to the next section, be sure you have
a first draft of your mission statement.

SET YOUR GOALS

So, you have a great idea for a non-profit. You have
filed the paperwork, received your 501(c) (3) determination
letter from the IRS, and you are ready to go! Now, you
just need to find some sponsors. Right? Wrong.

You're a thriving for-profit company, ready to plan
your first live event, and you are ready to go. Now you
just need a sponsor to cover your costs. Right? Wrong.

The foundation for any successful sponsorship program
is to know your goals. One of the organizations I currently
have the honor of working with has a $35 million vision
for her ministry. Some people have tried to discourage her
from achieving her vision, but I applaud her for having it!

It's difficult to reach any level of success without goals and milestones along the way help to measure your progress.

Her goal doesn't exist in her head. It is written down and has a few pictures associated with it to evoke the power of visual imagery. Written goals clarify our thinking, focus our efforts to keep us on target and provide an objective standard for measuring progress. Pictures tap into our emotions.

If you have managed projects in the for-profit world, you are probably familiar with the acronym SMART for defining goals.

- ✓ **S**pecific
- ✓ **M**easurable
- ✓ **A**ttainable
- ✓ **R**ealistic
- ✓ **T**ime-bound

"I want to raise money and secure sponsorship" is not a goal. It is a statement of desire or intent. "I want to raise $35 million" is getting closer. It is a little more specific and measurable, but it still sounds like wishful thinking. You have to be the judge of realistic and attainable based on your organization's maturity. How long will it take? One year? Ten years?

Now try, "Our organization will raise $35 million by December 31, 2015 to build a new center which will support senior citizens in the D.C. area." Does this meet the SMART criteria? Yes!

However, while this goal meets the SMART criteria, it is obviously too big to be of much use. It doesn't matter if the amount is $35 million or $150,000 you are going to break this larger objective into smaller SMART goals that form the foundation for your plan. For example, if your goal is to "raise $150,000 through sponsorships of our annual Gala on December 31, 2012" you will have several smaller, more focused goals such as:

✓ Secure $50,000 in table sponsorships by November 1, 2012
✓ Secure $50,000 through the sale of exclusive access VIP passes by November 30, 2012
✓ Secure $50,000 through the sale of premium placement event signage by November 15, 2012

Each of these goals will be broken down into smaller steps which will form an action or execution plan. Along with a due date, each step will also specify who is responsible for completing the step so that accountability is built into the execution process.

Think of it as a funnel. At the top of the funnel is the single overarching goal of your cause. As you move down the funnel, the goals become smaller, more specific and manageable until you are finally dealing with the actual steps of reaching the goal.

As you are building your plan, take a look at your team and their skills. What qualifies them to take ownership of a goal, beyond their willingness? Do they have a track record of success achieving that type of goal? What skills are needed to accomplish a goal? What are their skills? Do you have any skill gaps that need to be addressed? How will you close those gaps? If you don't address these issues early, you are setting your sponsorship up for failure.

> **SPONSORSHIP SECRET:** Don't treat the sponsor as though they are the "Bank of Mom and Dad", ready to write a check for your event just because they love your cause and you asked. Their objective is to be good stewards of their sponsorship funds. They will want to know more about your cause: what you hope to accomplish, who you will serve, how you plan to deliver your services and how you will measure success.

If your mission is to facilitate adoptions of foster children, then tell them what agencies you are working with, what types of counseling and adoption support services you offer, and share your best success stories. If you are new, be prepared to share your goals, with dates, and what you have accomplished to date so the prospective sponsors will know that you are measuring the effectiveness of your organization. If you managed to place 25 children with families last year, tout that success. Have a notebook and website which shows pictures of children waiting for homes and current photos of the families you helped.

Not only do they want to understand your overarching mission and how you plan to accomplish it, sponsors want to know if your team has the ability to accomplish your mission and the event or activity you are asking them to sponsor. Do they have the skills and experience necessary to be successful? Your plan should briefly address the qualifications of each person at critical junctures in the process. If you have a personnel gap, let them know how you plan to address it. Sponsors do not want to be involved in efforts that appear to be doomed to fail.

At the end of each of the Five Steps, I will present a few questions for you and your board, or organizing committee, to answer. If your organization is committee oriented, more than one person may be helping to answer the questions. A good practice is to have each person write down their answers, expectations and ideas independently. This will not only prevent the most persuasive and passionate individuals from swaying the group, but will require that everyone, at this level, have an intellectual connection and commitment to the success of the organization's sponsorship goals.

Here are a few questions to use as a guide when developing your goals:

1. What is our total fundraising goal for (year, event, etc.)?

2. How much of this amount do we want to secure from sponsors?

3. By when do we want to have these sponsorships secured?

4. What is our platform (vehicle for raising the funds, such as an event)?

5. What makes us credible?

6. Is this an appropriate event for us to seek sponsorship? If not, why?

RESEARCH THE OPTIONS

Your organization has goals, a mission statement, and is ready to continue to research your plan. When I recently started my new exercise program, I was surprised by how many options my local gym had. They had classes for everything, but not all of them resonated with my list of goals for the beginning of my exercise plan.

Just like I am passionate about this new exercise plan I've started, you are passionate about your vision and are prepared to invest the necessary time into building concrete relationships. Now, who do you approach and how do you price these packages?

This is one of the biggest challenges many organizations face. They either decide to approach everyone in town and get discouraged from the lack of response, or they become so paralyzed at the prospect of finding sponsors that they don't act at all. Perhaps this is why so many small non-profits and small businesses struggle to survive. The key is to target those prospects that are most likely to be interested in the same goals and objectives as your organization.

As you start this research process imagine yourself as a matchmaker. In the past, a matchmaker's financial success depended upon her ability to place two compatible people together, a task which required a great deal of homework. After all, a marriage was intended to last, and it didn't take long for word to spread if the marriages she arranged were unhappy. Your goal is to bring together two compatible parties for a long term relationship. To be successful, like the historical matchmaker, a great deal of homework is required from you too.

Here are some ways to develop a prospective sponsor list:

1. Make a list of the companies and corporations you would like to have as a sponsor

    a. Research their donation and sponsorship guidelines. Do you qualify? What do you need to do to qualify?

    b. What other organizations do they sponsor? Are they similar to yours? This is not an exercise in "stealing" another group's contributors. Most businesses and organizations sponsor multiple groups who share their values.

2. Make a list of other organizations that work with a clientele similar to yours. Find out what businesses and donors support them. Once again, you are not stealing sponsors, so don't worry.

3. Check out the foundation books at the library. While these are used primarily for people who are seeking grants, this is a valuable tool for finding the funding priorities of particular foundations and corporations. These books will also list some of the organizations that the company or foundation has supported in the past.

4. Who do you know? And not just you individually, but who do your board, staff and volunteers know? Pull out a piece of paper and make a list of people that you know who work for major corporations and then have your board or organizing committee do the same thing. Once you have the lists compiled, approach the individuals and ask if they know how sponsorships are handled at their company and if they'd be willing (as an employee of that company) to introduce you by email to that contact.

5. Examine the reputations of the prospective sponsors whenever possible. Make certain their business is compatible with your organization. For example, if you provide drug and alcohol counseling, don't ask the local beer distributor to sponsor your activities. They might actually be willing to do so, but sponsorships are built on relationships, and in this instance that relationship could be a stumbling block for the clientele you service. Also look at their sponsorship track record. Do the organizations they sponsor recognize them as a company who honors their commitments cheerfully and in a timely fashion?

6. The donor list. While many of the donors on your list may wish to remain donors, some might enjoy taking on an additional role as a sponsor. Ask them. You have nothing to lose.

Plan for Success

Now that you have successfully defined the terms of your organization and learned how to find prospective sponsors that share your same interests and values, your next step is to design a proposal package which highlights the benefits for the prospective sponsor. The ultimate key to designing a successful package is organization.

When asking a question, the prospective donor does not want to hear the answer, "I don't know." When you are at the proposal stage, you should know. Never approach a prospect with a half-finished idea. This implants the unfavorable perception in the prospective sponsor's mind that your organization is disorganized and probably not the best option for directing the company's allotted charitable funds. So, when you are approaching someone with a proposal, make sure to have all of the planning done and mapped out in a comprehensive manner. Make sure it makes sense, flows well and communicates what you intend.

The first thing you want to show in your proposal is the name of your organization, your mission statement, and the ways in which the goals and values of your organization are similar to the goals of your prospect. Along these lines, you can cite other organizations which the company has sponsored or given donations to which are similar to your organization. Doing this not only shows the prospect that they might want to advance the cause of your organization, but it also shows that you have taken the time to research and learn about their company. Knowing that you made an effort to familiarize yourself with their company and its goals always flatters and is a tool which can give your proposal the necessary edge it needs to be chosen above others.

Next, you must include a detailed description of the event for which you are seeking sponsorship, including:

- The event (what, when, where, how many and why)
- Volunteers (the team responsible for planning and execution)
- Available sponsorships types (advertising, tables, breaks, etc.)
- A working budget

A prospective sponsor wants to know, not only the goal of your event, but its scope and your organization's ability to acquire the necessary funding. Here is a list of questions that I use with my coaching clients when designing their sponsorship proposal packages.

QUESTIONS TO ASK BEFORE CREATING YOUR SPONSORSHIP PACKAGES/PROPOSALS

1. What is the name of your event?

2. When is your event?

3. What is the estimated budget for your event?

4. What is the estimated attendance for your event?

5. Where will the event take place?

6. Do you have any sponsors for this event? If so, how many and what amounts?

7. What is your fundraising goal?

8. How much of this goal would you like to secure in sponsorships?

9. What is the goal of your event?

10. Why are you doing this event? What do you need to accomplish?

11. What credibility factors do you have to attract sponsors?

12. What is your platform?

13. What are your core values?

14. Who are your ideal sponsors?

15. What types of exposure and benefits could your event provide sponsors?

16. What VIP experiences could you create for sponsors?

17. Is this a one time, recurring, or annual event?

18. Will sponsors receive exposure year round? If so, how?

19. Who is your audience?

Take this list and the 10-point Sponsor Value Checklist seriously. If you do not, I guarantee you will forget a question and miss a golden opportunity because you were unprepared. Do yourself the biggest favor right now by completing all the checklists and questions in this book as we go along. Start writing down your answers now!

> **SPONSORSHIP SECRET:** Keep in mind that as the sponsorship process has evolved, so have the rules of the game. Sponsorships aren't about you or the budgeting and marketing needs of your organization or event. Make your proposals a Win-Win situation.

Planning the Event

All the planning for your event must be done well in advance, to have the proper information for the proposal package. Since the primary goal of your event is to raise money for your organization, pricing is the biggest factor that must be considered. Everything involved in the event, the location, chairs, booths, a stadium, a sound system, advertisement signs, whatever your event might require, have costs associated with them. Your goal is to not only to make up the cost of holding the event, but to come out with a substantial profit to support your organization.

Pricing

There are many factors that go into pricing. Remember, the goal of your event is to make a profit. One way to make a profit is to get discounts for your needed supplies. Many venues will offer a discounted rate to non-profit organizations. You can also seek out discounted prices for other necessary supplies such as advertising signs. This way, you can put together your event for much less than it would cost a commercial business.

When calculating the prices for the levels of sponsorship you will present to your sponsors, you must calculate the actual value to the sponsor. This is just one of the ways that your organization makes money with these events, by basing price packages off of the event's market value rather than the actual cost. All these tactics will help you to make a profit.

When pricing your sponsorship opportunities, take into account any previous experience your organization has had in hosting these types of events. The previous years' budgets can serve as a guide for your current project.

Two key questions to consider when looking at past budgets:

1. Did you raise the desired amount of funds? If not, perhaps you asked too little for your sponsorships or were charging too much compared to the value the sponsor felt they were receiving in exchange. Adjust your prices accordingly.

2. Which sponsorships were most/least popular? How quickly did you sell out of the most popular sponsorships? What was undesirable about the least popular sponsorships? Adjust your sponsorship opportunities accordingly.

Past experience is a great means for determining present budgets.

If your organization or cause does not have any experience producing and hosting events, talk to organizations which are similar in size. Ask to look at their budgets for hosting similar events. This can at least give you a general idea of what to expect and a foundation from which you can build.

PACKAGE PERKS FOR SPONSORS

Questions 15-19 all deal with answering what kind of benefits your organization could provide to the prospective sponsor. While everything else in the package is important, it is often this last section that will secure the sponsorship. You have explained to the prospect all your organization's impressive goals and plans. Your next step is to show them all the ways in which they can benefit from this business relationship.

Question 15 asked you to consider what types of exposure and benefits your event could provide the sponsor. This is talking about the different types of measurable returns discussed in chapter one: event signage, web/print/radio and television advertising, access to mailing lists and opportunities for giveaways, to name a few.

These different types of returns take time and effort to obtain, so the more work you do in advance, the more your proposal will appeal to the prospective sponsor. Perhaps you have already acquired sponsorship from one of your states sports teams and one of the players on that team has agreed to speak at your event. You approached this prospect first because you knew that if a famous athlete agreed to speak at your event, then the media, especially a news program, would be more likely to provide coverage. After obtaining a promise of sponsorship from the team and the player, you approached a local news station who after hearing about your event's guest speaker, agreed to give your event five minutes of free airtime.

With these sponsorships already obtained, you can offer your current sponsorship prospect the opportunity to receive television advertising. Now, it is important that you make sure to follow through on this promise. So, if you know that part of your airtime will include a section of the athlete's speech, you could offer to place a banner with the sponsor's name behind the speaker.

Hopefully this gives you an idea of the wide variety of benefits you can provide sponsors, as well as an idea of the extensive pre-planning required to successfully market your event to sponsors. Remember, a lot of your success will be dependent upon the amount of effort you are willing to exert.

The next question, "What VIP experiences could you create for sponsors," refers to any special offers that can be made to a limited number of people. For example, perhaps you have a famous individual speaking at your event, or maybe a popular entertainer has agreed to perform. You can prearrange agreements to allow a limited number of executives to meet with the celebrity after the event. This allows certain sponsors a once in a lifetime opportunity for them to meet this person. These are the types of measures that you can take to greatly increase the appeal of your proposal package and are also great ways to increase the funds you are able to raise.

Another key reason for VIP experiences is that most large corporations are already used to the hospitality suites and probably have more free movie and rodeo tickets than they know what to do with. A true VIP experience is something that they won't find anywhere else.

Several years ago, while working with a concert promoter, we created a package that offered the presenting sponsor the opportunity to have dinner with the headlining artist, a photo meet and greet and back stage passes for the evening. Most concerts have meet and greet passes to give away, but we really set the bar with this event. We even had sponsors *fighting* over the opportunity to be the presenting sponsor for a future event. The once in a lifetime opportunity to take their families to these private, backstage dinners with the artist was an overwhelming success to say the least!

You must also ask yourself "Is this a one time, recurring, or annual event?" This is an important factor that all sponsors want to know. After all, the sponsor will want to know if they are writing a one-time check or making a year round investment in the community. An example of a one-time event would be a cleanup project after a natural disaster where you collect sponsorships for groups of volunteers to assist in cleanup and rebuilding of an area devastated by a tornado or flood.

On the other hand, providing funding for a project such as the building of an activities center has lasting effects and would be considered a long-term investment in the community. Maybe the large event for which you are asking for sponsorship help is an annual event. You would want to make the prospective sponsor aware of this so that they can have the opportunity to pledge for consecutive years. Even if they don't pledge more than one year of support, by letting them now that the event is annual and by giving them a positive experience, they will be likely to consider your organization in the future.

As pointed out by question 18, "Will sponsors receive exposure year round?" you need to determine if this is truly the case. If so, the "how," is very important for sponsors to know. They also need to know whether the event is a one-time deal or long-term commitment. If it is a long-term commitment, they must be aware of any benefits they will receive for their extensive commitment and presence.

For example, perhaps your non-profit provides technological education for the adult community and you need to build a new computer room. That room can be dedicated and named after the individual, or company that provided the funds and a plaque can be placed outside the door acknowledging the sponsor. This is an opportunity for year round exposure since everyone entering the room will be able to view the plaque with the sponsor's name.

Anyone who has entered a museum or a sports arena has likely seen this type of long-term exposure. Plaques acknowledging sponsors can be found throughout the various exhibits of a museum and sports arenas often have billboards and posters for sponsors which remain in the building year round. Public parks are another example. Have you ever sat on a bench that had an engraving or plaque reading, "This bench is dedicated in the honor of (name of individual)?" Or perhaps the bench is dedicated to a company. This is an example of continual exposure since that sign is constantly being viewed.

Finally, as the last question suggests, it is important to consider your audience. Before pitching a proposal idea, you need to know to whom you are speaking. What company are they representing? What are the values of your sponsor? What types of advertising would be most beneficial and appealing to them? What type of special benefits might you offer that they would be likely to accept? In other words, you need to find the best possible way to present your idea to a specific sponsor.

You also need to consider the audience your event will attract. Are the people attending your event likely to include members of the prospective sponsor's target audience? For example, if your event focuses on at-risk youth and is likely to attract mostly youth and parents, this is not the target audience for a sponsor such as a large tobacco or alcohol company. However, if your event is a sports tournament to raise money for building a fitness center, the collective audience might be more in line with the target audience for a sponsor such a large gym or sporting goods store. These are all factors that must be considered in advance for you to make an appealing and successful package for your prospective sponsor.

Repeat sponsors should always be given some extra consideration and recognition. When creating a package for someone that has sponsored you in the past, always begin by acknowledging their generous contribution, thanking them for their support, and letting them know that a continued relationship would be highly valued by your organization. Treatment of previous sponsors will be discussed in more detail in the next chapter, but it is important that such acknowledgment be included in a proposal package.

> **SPONSORSHIP SECRET:** Learn the values and marketing objectives of your potential sponsors and then make sure your proposals match their values and their sponsorship and/or marketing goals.

Now that we've set our goals and completed our self-assessment and research, we're ready to create our prospective sponsor packages. Your package should be no longer than 15-pages and should be packaged in a professional manner, addressed to the person with whom you are speaking.

Here is a list of items your proposal should include:

✓ **Executive Summary.** An executive summary is a letter from the director or board that introduces you organization and the event for which you are seeking sponsors. This includes the name of your organization, the people you serve, and your mission statement.

✓ **Overview of the project or event.** As has been mentioned above, you must provide a clear description of your event, including a budget, the scope of the event, and the event's purpose.

✓ **Market Research** on the event. Give facts that build the credibility of your event.

✓ **Promotional Plan.** This includes a description of any marketing you have in place for the event, such as web, print, radio, and television sources and any other means by which you can market their company through your event.

✓ **Testimonials** of past guests, clients, and sponsors.

✓ **Sponsor Benefits.** This is where you describe the different levels of sponsorship. With signage, for example, you can have a map which shows the different locations where signs will be placed.

On this map you can have marked the prime locations for signs (such as behind a speaker) which can be purchased at a higher price than less visible locations.

✓ **THE ASK.** The final part of the package is a request. You can do a lot of work and put together a great package but miss an opportunity simply because you did not ask for a commitment. You should ask the prospective sponsor at which level they would like to sponsor the event and have a sponsorship commitment sheet on which to record their commitment to your organization.

After you have created your proposal, it's time to examine the proposal from the sponsor's point of view. I have repeated the Sponsor Value Checklist from earlier in the book, below. Use these questions to evaluate your proposal and shore up any weak points.

1. Does the sponsorship match our values and the market we are trying to reach?

2. Will this gain us exposure to new customers within our target market?

3. How much media exposure will we receive and how does that compare to our media buys?

4. Is there a possibility for a multi-year agreement?

5. What comps are we given?

6. Who are some of the previous sponsors?

7. Would a competitor sponsor the event should we decline?

8. What is the track record of success for this organization?

9. What media exposure will there be?

10. Are there any celebrities or politicians affiliated with the event?

EXERCISE

Now that your plan is ready, it's time to put it into action! There are several levels to this process. For instance, you must find out the means of contact that the prospective sponsor prefers. Some companies will prefer to be contacted via phone or email before they will meet with you in person. Often, companies will require the proposal package to be sent for consideration by the board and either make a decision for sponsorship based on your proposal or ask for a face-to-face meeting. It is essential to find out the means by which the prospective sponsor operates so that you do not offend them in any way.

The purpose of a pitch, whether it occurs via email, the telephone, or through a face-to-face interaction, is to make your offer enticing enough that you will receive an offer to meet with a decision maker in person. When a representative from a sponsorship department agrees to meet with you, this is a great sign! These people have small teams and are managing large amounts of sponsorship dollars, so they don't like to waste their time.

In many cases, getting the meeting will take more than one encounter on your part, but don't get frustrated with the gatekeepers (those receptionists, secretaries, and human resource employees who stand between you and the decision maker.) That person is not the enemy; they are simply doing the job they have been paid to do. Instead, this is a key person to begin building a relationship with. Be courteous, appreciative and personal. Gatekeepers are a fountain of information and can help smooth the way to the decision maker, or they can toss your proposal in the trash. What happens largely depends on how well you handle this initial contact.

KEYS TO SUCCESS IN SPONSORSHIP MEETINGS:

1. Do not be anxious. You may feel nervous, especially if this is your first pitch. Focus on your goal. You believe in your organization. You know that you have great things to offer your sponsors and that this will be a mutually beneficial relationship. All you have to do is convey this to him.

2. Excitement is good when presenting your idea, but it is important not to become so excited that you forget about the time entirely.

3. Do not take more people than absolutely necessary. Only take those key contacts who can contribute maximum value to the meeting.

4. Plan and practice your presentation. Prepare your information in advance so that you can properly convey your message within the existing time slot. Know the timing and always allow enough time for 5 – 10 minutes of questions at the end of your presentation.

5. Do not assume anything. If you cannot answer a question, set a time frame to provide the potential sponsor an answer. Once the time frame is set, be sure to follow through.

Armed with your completed proposal and a presentation, you are now ready to begin meeting with your prospects. But who? The next chapter will help you weed out your prospects so that your efforts are more efficient and result in a "Yes" more often than a "No."

There is everything you know and there is everything that happens. When the two do not line up, you make a choice.

— MITCH ALBOM
FOR ONE MORE DAY

CHAPTER 4

VALUE IN — VALUE OUT

O nce again, while you are looking for money for an upcoming fundraiser or someone to sponsor a scholarship to a worthy event, what you want is more than a one-time-only interaction. You want to develop lasting relationships. One way to sum up the process of developing lasting relationships is with the acronym V.A.S.T.

V — Values

A — Attitude

S — Service

T — Trust

VALUES: Choose to meet with prospects that have the same core values as your organization. Various questions we've covered earlier attempt to get to your core values. To discover their values, a great place to check is their corporate website or the websites of other non-profits they sponsor. While values may seem like limiting factors to some, conducting a screening exercise for prospects will save you time, money and keep you from becoming discouraged. More importantly, it will help you to connect with the prospects that share your core values.

ATTITUDE: When you approach prospects, do so with a gracious, humble attitude. You should be very proud of the work your organization does, but be aware that the prospect does not owe you anything. Don't go in with the attitude that your prospects are under any obligation to you or that, if they don't sponsor this particular event, you should automatically cross them off the list.

If they show interest, but have already committed their funding for the year, then find out when those decisions are made. It is not uncommon for a company to plan their corporate sponsorships a year in advance as part of the annual budget. What if they aren't interested at the moment or simply say there wasn't a match? Take this opportunity to find out how you could better package your information to be a fit for their funding. Ask questions and always have the mindset of a coachable student. Most people in the sponsorship world will tell you exactly what they're looking to fund, if you'll only listen. If you think about it, ask if they know of a company that might be a better funding match for you. Lastly, be respectful and appreciative of any and all time they give you. Be sure to follow up with them as this could possibly be the first steps towards a new working relationship.

SERVICE: Can fall into two very distinct categories. The service an organization provides and the leadership style of its teams. If your organization is service based, does it serve a clientele the prospect is also interested in? If the prospect is a business, are the people in your target group also in his customer base? If so, this may provide him with a double incentive to sponsor your function.

When it comes to your leadership, are they servant leaders? Aside from the obvious marketing benefits, people in the sponsorship world want to know that their donation or funding is making a difference and extending the reach of their brand. Will your leadership team effectively reflect and represent their brand? Does your leadership team serve on the front line? Are they involved in the actual volunteer work and securing of sponsorships? Sponsors like to see that your leadership is interwoven throughout the day to day operations of your organization, and not just the board room. Having 100% board involvement is also key when securing any grants or sponsorships.

As you screen the prospect, notice if they are walking the talk in their service. What are their customers saying? What do other organizations they sponsor notice about their treatment of employees and the organization's volunteers? If they don't walk the talk, they might not be a good fit for you.

Trust: The glue that will cement the relationships with your sponsors. Be transparent and trustworthy with your prospects, both before and after they have made a commitment. They need to know that if they are sponsoring an event, it will occur in the manner you have described and the funds raised will be spent for the stated purpose. If the money is designated to purchase aids to assist the blind, don't rationalize spending part of the funds on an emergency plumbing issue instead. The organization has a legal and moral obligation to the donors.

This doesn't mean that problems won't occur along the way, requiring some adjustment in your plans. Perhaps you are seeking sponsors for a theater night. Sponsorships have been coming in for a price of $500. In return, these individuals and organizations will receive tickets for a play, refreshments and other gifts. Then you receive notice that the theater in question will be unable to host the event that night due to a water main break. Make adjustments in your plans by either changing the dates or the venue and notify your sponsors immediately.

So far, it sounds like the burden is all on you. However, trust is a two-way street. No relationship, either personal or corporate, can exist if only one of the parties is trustworthy. Do your homework and vet the sponsor! Check with other organizations they sponsor to see if they have a history of honoring their commitments.

If a sponsor has agreed to underwrite the cost of a venue for your event, it can be disastrous if he pulls out at the last minute. One way to prevent this last minute glitch, is to put date expectations in your proposal. If the rent for your August gala must be paid by July 1, set an earlier date for the sponsorship deadline in your proposal. Setting the expectation that the money must arrive by June 1 gives your organization an opportunity to find alternate funding if a sponsor bails out. It also avoids potential misunderstandings between you and the sponsor and allows the sponsor to budget accordingly. Once the money arrives, trustworthiness on the part of the non-profit requires that the funds be set aside in a separate account until needed for the designated expenditures. Do NOT co-mingle the sponsorship money paid in advance with the general operating funds where it can unintentionally be used for other needs.

It can be tempting to accept any sponsor who might be willing to write a check, particularly if you are feeling desperate. Unfortunately, like most marriages of convenience, they often end in a messy divorce if you ignore VAST. You don't need to be involved with a sponsor that can ruin your reputation before you've had a chance to establish it.

I've learned that people will forget what you said, people will forget what you did, but people will never forget how you made them feel.

— MAYA ANGELOU

CHAPTER 5

THE REAL RELATIONSHIP BEGINS

YOU'VE CLOSED THE DEAL WITH A SPONSOR,
CONGRATULATIONS! NOW WHAT?

At this point your sponsorship planning is rocketing forward. You have your sponsors lined up, checks or pledges in hand, and you are ready to move on to the actual event itself. Perhaps you even have a committee of staff and volunteers in place that will be doing the actual set-up of the event. Can your sponsorship campaign go on autopilot now?

Not hardly. Remember, this is not just about getting a one-time check and moving on. Sponsorship is built upon relationships, and those must be nurtured to secure future sponsorships. Also, it is up to you to make certain that pledges are paid, money is handled, and promises are kept. This requires accountability, implementation, and maintenance.

THE AGREEMENT

Creating the actual sponsorship agreement can be a tedious process, especially if you are dealing with a large corporation. Most large corporations will suggest having their attorneys draft the sponsorship agreements and while this is not always bad, be sure to have your attorney or legal counsel review the document before signing it.

Whether your team or the corporation's team drafts the agreement, make sure it is as detailed as possible since this document will be the foundation to creating a successful sponsorship relationship with each other. I'm not suggesting the agreement turn into a 40-page legal manuscript, but provide enough detail that both parties are comfortable with the final contract.

While this is not a complete list, here are some of the terms and conditions that should be listed, defined, and agreed to in the contract:

- ✓ Who is agreeing to sponsorship (you and them)
- ✓ What is being sponsored and what are the terms of the sponsorship
- ✓ What are the milestones set in the sponsorship
- ✓ What benefits or comps is the sponsor receiving
- ✓ What are the financial components of the sponsorship? How much is due when?
- ✓ Include a conflict of interest policy
- ✓ Include a non-disclosure agreement and confidentiality agreement
- ✓ What is the process for dispute resolution?
- ✓ List any other special conditions of the sponsorship

Once again, whether your team or the legal team with your sponsor drafts the agreement, have your attorney review all documents before signing them.

SPONSOR ACCOUNTABILITY

As in every relationship, there are two sides of accountability. In some instances your prospects will not actually hand you a check; often they will make a pledge to provide the funds at a future date. It is now your responsibility to make certain the pledge is fulfilled, and to do so in a tactful, courteous manner. The last thing you want is to come across as a bill collector.

Here are some steps you can take to follow up with those who have pledged their support but have not remitted the funds.

1. Send a gracious thank you note for the pledge of sponsorship. Since you have used the steps above to develop your sponsorship package, you have already included the due date for each level of sponsorship. This was a vital piece of information for the prospect. However, don't assume that the entire packet will make its way to the bookkeeping department or that the deadline will be remembered. In the text of your letter thank the sponsor for their level of sponsorship (name the exact thing they plan on doing), then state the amount pledged in $_____$, to be paid by _____ (date funds are required).

2. Include a second paragraph which repeats the purpose of the event or activity that is being sponsored. For example, "Your sponsorship will make possible our "adoption field day event," an

activity which will bring foster children in need of a loving home together with families who are looking for a child to adopt.

3. In the thank you note, include a remittance voucher and a self-addressed envelope. This can be a small, envelope-size form if you wish.

4. If the pledge does not have a deadline for six months, you certainly don't want to wait until the last minute to ask for the money, yet you should not send monthly statements. Make certain the initial thank you note with the remittance voucher is sent, and then do not bother the sponsor for the funds until the deadline approaches. You can, however, add that particular sponsor to a newsletter / update that you can send to all of the sponsors on the list. This keeps your organization and activity visible.

5. A pre-event update letter is only needed when there is a significant amount of time between acquiring the sponsors and the date of the event. This can be a short, newsy update on exciting developments for the upcoming event. Perhaps you have received a commitment from an exciting keynote speaker or band since the time your sponsorship package was developed. If so, this is a great item to share that will maintain the sponsor's interest while at the same time serving as a gentle reminder of the pledge.

6. Within a couple of weeks of the deadline for a pledge, you can send out a short letter once again thanking the sponsor for their pledge and letting them know that a payment voucher and envelope have been enclosed for their convenience.

ORGANIZATIONAL ACCOUNTABILITY

Once the sponsorships are in, the burden of accountability lies completely on the organization and this responsibility extends to several areas.

You are always accountable for living up to the mission statement and vision of the organization. The first step in soliciting sponsors, donors, clients and community involvement begins with defining who and what the organization is and what services it will provide. These same assertions are what drew the sponsors to you. A cruise ship line does not sell tickets for a two-week trip around the Mediterranean Sea, load up the passengers and luggage, just to then change course and spend five days in the Pacific instead. If that happened, the company would quickly go out of business. All of the travelers would be lining up, demanding a refund, filing lawsuits, and telling everyone (including media) about their unreliable and unethical treatment.

That does not mean that an organization cannot, at some time, make a determined shift in its focus; it most certainly can. If this is done, however, it needs to be done only after careful deliberation and notification. All donors and sponsors should be notified well in advance of the proposed move and given the opportunity to withdraw their support if the new mission statement is no longer compatible with their donation focus.

Once the sponsorship packages have been given out, the focus of the sponsored event should not change. If the event is a 5k run, it needs to remain a 5k run. If the funds being raised are to provide scholarships for low-income, at-risk students living in failing school districts to attend your private academy, then every single penny of profit raised by the event should go to that particular scholarship fund, period.

If your goal is to raise $20,000 and you actually raise $30,000, then put all of that money into the designated cause. This is a matter of integrity.

There may be occasions where you actually do raise more money than is required for a certain item. Consider this when you are putting your packages together.

For example, maybe you need to raise $25,000 to replace the roof on your neighborhood activity center. Chances are very likely that there are a few other repairs or upgrades that need to be done. Or perhaps the activity center could really use some new athletic equipment as well. If this were the case, make a provision for this reality, right up front.

To illustrate, "Funds raised at the Parker Community Center's Annual Theater Gala will be used to replace the activity center roof and to worn out athletic equipment."

Another matter of financial integrity is to not misuse, or "borrow" funds given in advance for a sponsored event. This money should be set aside in a separate savings or checking account that is only used for the event. Do not mislead your sponsor by asking for funds several months in advance of their use. If a company has given you $15,000 to pay for the rent for the event venue six months in advance, but instead you let that money draw interest for the next six months, your integrity will be shot and you may face legal consequences. Do not divert event funds to other purposes. If you borrow part of a sponsor's designated funds and then cannot come up with the rent, causing you to have to move or cancel the event, you can count on plenty of cold shoulders in the future.

An additional step in transparency, consider is having a complete audit of the organization's books done on an annual or bi-annual basis by a CPA or accounting firm. Many foundations and larger corporations actually ask to see a recent audit report before they will commit to becoming a sponsor. Just as your organization has an obligation to use sponsorship funds properly, the sponsor feels an obligation to be a good steward of its charitable giving. This is not usually required if the sponsor is an individual, a smaller company, or if the amount of the sponsorship is relatively small.

In addition to assuring that the event occurs in the time and manner promised, that the purpose of the event doesn't change, and that the funds are carefully monitored, it is absolutely vital to keep the promises made to the sponsors. Set up a database that lists every sponsorship opportunity, the sponsor that chooses that opportunity, and the benefits which that sponsorship carries. Also include a column for extra notes or agreements that have been made. This does not mean that your organization will treat sponsors unequally; you won't, but you need to be flexible. What if a sponsor is willing to pay a bit more for something additional that you may have not thought to offer? Can you be open for that?

For example, your organization is holding a benefit concert at a local amphitheater. You offer all of the traditional sponsorship levels including venue rent, signage (at various prices depending upon location), and advertising in the printed program, guest boxes, and concessions. These offers are for a set rate, and everyone who pays that rate gets the same benefits. A neighborhood corporation has agreed to sponsor one of the guest boxes, but notices that you have not provided a sponsorship for parking attendants. Perhaps you had originally planned to use volunteers for this task, but the company offers to provide employee volunteers for this job as long as their employees are allowed to wear orange safety vests with their name and logo at their expense.

Why not accept that offer? In fact, you can follow it up with a suggestion that, for an additional fee, you can provide sandwich board signs at the entrances to the parking lot which say, "Parking attendants courtesy of the Corporation." Just make certain that the fee they pay covers more than just the cost of the sign boards. Everyone who is driving to the event will see the signs, so these offer greater exposure than the signs in the back corner of the theater, yet they are not as desirable as the signs at the front gate. A guest will spend less time looking at the parking lot sign then he will standing in line to enter the event. Make certain that these requirements are noted.

Good record keeping also helps you to not oversell. Know how many signs or sponsorships you have allocated for any given event. If the entrance has room for only four signs, don't sell sponsorships for eight gate signs.

This seems really basic, but if multiple people are approaching various sponsors, they need to have a central point of contact for updates. Put in your package that a limited number of each type of sponsorship is available, and that they are available on a first come—first serve basis. Make certain that sponsorship records are updated daily and that the people out meeting with prospects have the most current information available before making calls each day.

If your organization is inexperienced at acquiring sponsors, you may find the prospect of overbooking rather unrealistic, but even first time events encounter this possibility. The more established your non-profit event is, the greater the chances are that you may need to deal with such a contingency. So what happens when a sponsorship check arrives for that fifth gate sign and you only have room for four signs? This requires a personal phone call. A protocol should be developed to make the call effective.

Here are some suggestions for overbooking protocol:

- Thank the sponsor for his consideration. Let him know how much it means to your organization that he desires to partner with you.

- Next, tell the sponsor that there were only four of those premium positions available, and unfortunately, these had all been taken before his check arrived.

- Let him know about other options available, list them along with the associated sponsorship fees.

- Give him a choice. Ask him if one of the reduced fee positions would be agreeable. If he is unhappy with those choices, ask if any of the other types of sponsorships would be of interest.

- If he is willing to accept a lower cost opportunity, give him a choice of receiving a refund of the price difference or of gaining an additional benefit for the difference in price, making certain that the additional benefit is comparable in cost. For example, let's say the cost difference is $1,000 and this is the same price you are charging for two tickets to the event or for a quarter page ad in the written program. Let him know what the choices are and then let him make the choice. This is part of the relationship building process.

- Once again, give him a choice. This may sound redundant, but relationships won't flourish unless both parties feel respected and valued. Do NOT just send him a letter telling him that he did not get what he wanted, and that you have arbitrarily made the choice to move his sign to a different location, keep his money, and then send him some other benefit as a consolation prize. If he wants the financial difference refunded to him, do so cheerfully. But if you have options available to offer, the sponsor will probably be happy to accept the alternative.

IMPLEMENTATION: ROADWAY TO SUCCESS

Effective implementation is vitally important, not only to the success of the event itself but also to maintaining good relationships with all of the parties involved; sponsors, staff, volunteers, board, media, the community you serve, and of course, members of the sponsorship committee. A smoothly run campaign brings people back; a train wreck drives them away.

THE TEAM

One of the keys to implementing a successful sponsorship drive and event is to start early and have a great team in place. Just as every orchestra needs a conductor, this team needs to have a chairperson or team leader, as well as members with administrative skills, and people to solicit the sponsorships.

HERE IS A LIST OF TRAITS DESIRED FOR EACH ROLE:

SPONSORSHIP TEAM LEADER

- Strong organizational skills
- Some knowledge of every facet of the sponsorship process
- Leadership skills—a leader, not a driver
- A track record of building relationships
- Boldness—not afraid to contact and meet with prospects

ADMINISTRATIVE SUPPORT

- Strong organizational skills
- Computer skills—able to maintain sponsor database
- Research skills—ability to gather background data on prospective sponsors
- Good written communication skills—if this person will be drafting the correspondence
- Good verbal / telephone skills—ability to interface with sponsors, leader, organization and other team members

SPONSORSHIP SOLICITORS

- Great people skills
- Not easily discouraged
- Enthusiastic
- Once again, boldness. Cannot be afraid to make the contact
- Relationship builders
- Able to commit time

This list covers essential requirements for the team, though the size and structure of the group may vary depending upon your purpose. Most non-profits have (or should have) regular staff members dedicated to development It is beneficial if one person is dedicated to the job of developing sponsorships for the organization. This person may be the only person involved in seeking sponsors for smaller needs, such as website development and maintenance, camp scholarships or small events. Larger events will require a larger team.

Part of the team planning process is to determine a labor budget. Reasonable time estimates should be established for each function so that you know your labor requirements. If you are using volunteers, don't expect them to dedicate forty hours a week to the cause. Set a minimum time availability requirement for the task they will be assigned to, and confirm each volunteer's time commitment. By doing this, the volunteer and the team leader will have a mutual understanding of expectations. This helps to prevent volunteer burnout, and lets the team leader know how many people to recruit for each task.

IMPLEMENTATION SUPPORT TOOLS

Develop a timeline based upon actual deadlines quoted from vendors to ensure deadlines are met and promises fulfilled. This should include current quotes from the vendors, and not on a best guess or even on the schedule adopted last year. This timeline is a critical planning and implementation tool and should be posted in an area accessible to the entire team. The timeline becomes a guide for charting progress and keeping important deadlines—like the lead time for getting the signage orders in—from being overlooked.

Establish a database that records all of the sponsor's names, types, what they have committed to, and the benefits they require. You should be able to sort this data by type of sponsorships and track the progress made. For example, if one of the sponsorship levels is signage, each sponsor will probably be giving you a layout for the sign, including their name and logo. In your data base, you can track when the information is due from the sponsor (preferably a few days before the printer deadline), record the date sponsor input is received, when the materials are taken to the printer, and when the signs will be picked up by the non-profit. By monitoring the timeline and the database you can prevent things from slipping through the cracks. If it is only a few days before materials are due to the printer and you don't have signage information for one of your sponsors, you will know in plenty of time to place a reminder phone call.

Assign someone, possibly the administrative team member, to track the vendors. Even though you received a quote six months ago that stated only two weeks were needed to print all of the signs, this needs to be confirmed in advance. It is entirely possible that business is now booming for your vendor and he will need a full month to deliver your signs. These phone calls should be made with a gracious, cooperative spirit. Make your vendor feel that you are working as a team to produce a great product. Don't make him feel so hassled that if he ever works with you again his bid will double.

KEEPING THE SPONSOR IN THE LOOP

Building the capacity of your non-profit depends upon finding sponsors who will be champions of your organization for more than just one event. While there will always be some businesses or foundations who limit their involvement to one sponsorship for one event every two or three years, the majority have the capacity to become partners of your organization. Building this base will add stability to your organization and allow you to continually expand your sponsor base. Doing this requires developing relationships. Without this base, every event will be started at the ground floor, constantly trying to replace the support from the previous year instead of spending some time nurturing the relationships while still having time available to continue meeting new prospects.

One vital step nurturing a relationship is to keep the sponsor in the loop, especially during the event process. No, they don't want a weekly activity report (though your board might). The sponsors are busy with their businesses and lives. They also don't what to feel that your interest in them ended the minute you got your hands on the check. As covered earlier, send thank you notes, and updates of any significance that will help maintain their interest. If someone is sponsoring signage, drop a note or make a call when the sign comes in from the printer. Let them know how great the finished product looks and that you look forward to seeing them at the event. If no one from the sponsor will be attending, make certain you tell them that you will provide a photo of their sign at the event.

The old adage that a picture is worth a thousand words is very true. Do NOT forget to have a photographer at the event. Make certain this is someone, perhaps a staff member or very trustworthy volunteer, who is designated to take photos of all sponsor-related activities, tables, signs, plaques, etc. Also, take pictures that show people enjoying the event.

Follow up with a post-event recap for all of the sponsors. Let them know how effective the event was and thank them once again for their partnership. Make these contacts personal; so don't start a letter with "Dear valued sponsor." If they are so valued, they should be called by name. Also include their level of sponsorship and photos of the event. If applicable, have testimonials from some of the people in your service target area who have been helped. End the correspondence with a statement about how you value their assistance and hope to continue partnering with them in the future.

DEVELOPING LONG-TERM RELATIONSHIPS WITH SPONSORS

A good donor / sponsor software database is also an essential tool. Some organizations design their own database when first starting out, but there are a number of great software tools available that allow you to record specific information about each sponsor, build a variety of mailing lists, log all sponsor contacts and activity, and so forth. Some of these databases have note sections for recording information from meetings and phone calls. For example, if your contact mentions an upcoming vacation or the birth of a new child, record that information. The next time you call, you can look at the record and then ask them about their vacation or how the new baby is doing. This makes the person feel remembered and valued. Even if your sponsor is a big company, your connection value is as a human being, and that is the level where relationships are built.

Building great, long-term relationships requires letting your sponsors connect with you, your mission and your clientele. A monthly or bi-monthly newsletter is a great opportunity to tout your success stories and highlight your sponsor's contributions. Don't make this your monthly plea for more money. Include fun, positive articles and notices of upcoming activities. Let the newsletter be something your sponsor will look forward to receiving. These days you don't even have to spend money on printing and postage because of the internet, so NO EXCUSES!

If your articles appear in any news media outlets, highlight that publicity. Mention it in your newsletter, post a video clip of the TV segment on your website, or make copies of the newspaper articles to send to your sponsors. It is important for them to know that the media is aware of you and your work. This makes the advertising benefits they can receive with on-going or future sponsorships appear even more attractive.

Invest time on building up the relationship. Be willing to meet for lunch or coffee. You don't want to be a nag or make your contact groan when they see your number on the caller ID, so it is important to vary how you reach out and connect. One month you may place a phone call; the next time you might sent a postcard or a copy of a news article about your organization with a handwritten greeting. You can also offer an annual sponsor appreciation night when sponsors can have dinner, meet some of your clientele, view the facility or in some other way connect with the organizations. Remember, you are looking for sponsors who will become long-term friends and champions of your cause.

*You can't build a reputation on what
you're going to do.*

— Henry Ford

Chapter 6

Measuring Effectiveness

Einstein once defined insanity as "doing the same thing over and over again and expecting different results." This seems obvious, but your organization or cause could be in danger of doing just that if you don't take the time to debrief after an event. In fact, this is something the development segment of your organization should do on a periodic basis. If you have just completed a major sponsorship activity, make certain to debrief your team shortly after the event, while memories are sharpest and you can gain the most insight on the effectiveness of the sponsorship process. Measuring effectiveness after a major event falls into three categories; monetary effectiveness, the event itself, and the progress made in gaining sponsors and building relationships.

HERE ARE SOME FACTORS YOU WILL WANT TO ASSESS:

MONETARY EFFECTIVENESS

1. How accurate was your budget? Compare the budget to the actual expenditures. Were there unexpected costs that need to be taken into consideration next time? How effective were you at soliciting discounts

and donations to cover the cost of items that were not part of the sponsorship packages?

2. How accurate was your labor budget? Did you have adequate human resources to complete the planning, sponsorship campaign, event set-up, production, tear-down and follow up? Where there any gaps? Were some of the people and tasks mismatched? Are the team members and volunteers suffering from burn-out or excited by the smooth execution and accomplishments of the event?

3. Did you reach your sponsorship and fundraising goals?

4. How effective was the pricing on your sponsorship packages? Were they priced appropriately? Get feedback from the team now, while everything is fresh, so any packages which need to be revamped for next time are evaluated.

EVENT EFFECTIVENESS

1. Did the event itself run smoothly? Gather input from those working the actual event and see if they can offer "lessons learned" about what went well, what could be better, and what needs to be changed. These notes will be very helpful next time.

2. Did the event meet attendance goals? Solicit feedback from attendees and those who worked the

event. What did they hear guests saying? How did the guests hear about your event? This might be a good question to ask at the entrance or when selling tickets. In that way you can judge which advertising venues were the most effective.

3. If the event was a community activity, was the community involved? If members of the community you serve were present, how well were they able to interact with the community and sponsors?

4. If this was a community event with a particular purpose, like finding summer jobs for at-risk kids or connecting foster kids with adoptive parents, do you have any success stories?

5. If this is an annual event, how did it compare to previous years? Take a look at attendance, fundraising, and sponsorship to see if these are holding steady, trending up or trending down. If there is a downward trend in these areas for some time, you may need to change the event or venue.

6. How was the media coverage? Gather information about the venues you were able to gain access to and those you were not successful in reaching. Record any lessons learned in this process as well. For instance, if you discovered a new radio venue, but just missed the forty-five day advance notice required for community announcements, then collect that data so you will be able to tap into this resource in the future. Have any relationships

begun between any members of the team and members of the media? Is there a contact that could be useful in the future? Your development department should keep files on all of the media outlets with this type of information.

SPONSORSHIP EFFECTIVENESS

1. Were all of the promises made to the sponsors kept? If there were any glitches, analyze what the cause was and how the problem was handled. Don't let anything slip through the cracks.

2. Did you meet your sponsorship goals? Whether this was the first time you have had a sponsored event or you're old pros at the process, gather input about what worked and what seemed to be a challenge with the team that solicited prospective sponsors. Review every sponsor and note in their file information regarding why they chose to sponsor this particular activity and if there is anything in their funding guidelines that only allows them to participate on a periodic basis.

3. Debrief the successful sponsorship solicitations. What approach was used? Why did that person / company / foundation choose to become a sponsor?

4. Debrief the unsuccessful sponsorship solicitations. If a prospect turned down the opportunity, was a reason given? Did you have insufficient or inaccurate information about their funding guidelines? If the

reason for the rejection was because of a missed deadline, then make certain to record the due date for submitting sponsorship requests.

5. Have any sponsors indicated an interest in partnering again with your non-profit?

Advertising, sales promotion and sponsorship all have very unique relationships with one another. Just because people are spending less on sales and promotion one year does not mean that sponsorships have taken a dive as well. Do your best to keep yourself updated with current information on trends in your industry. At the very least it can make for some meaningful banter with a sponsor about the state of the industry.

CREATING VALUE

Your sponsors have a vested interest in the success of the event, and they deserve a follow-up. Nothing can spoil a relationship faster than to feel used and unappreciated. They signed on to your event, in part because of shared values, but in general because they had a genuine belief in your organization or cause and a desire to help the community you serve. They also hope to reap some benefits for their own organization during the process as well. They want to gain access to the contacts within your organization and service community, and to gain increased public awareness of their own enterprise through the advertising opportunities from the event. Remember, sponsorship is a mutually beneficial relationship.

After the event, you still have an opportunity to increase the benefits to both your organization and to the sponsors. Write up small news stories, with photos, of the event. Let the community know about the wonderful programs being helped by a fun activity that occurred thanks to the generous sponsorship of X, Y and Z sponsors. Send versions of the story out to different media. This is the type of article a community paper is likely to publish. When you get that follow up article in a paper, make copies of it to send to your sponsors. This will let them know that they are still reaping the benefits of becoming partners with your great organization.

Before updating the sponsors you need to determine the value to both your organization and to the sponsor. It will be important to tell the sponsors about the money raised or community service provided, so they know that the event they sponsored effectively accomplished its purpose. No one wants to continue to support a failing enterprise. This is where you share the success stories. For example, if your charity is a golden retriever rescue organization and you held an event to raise money and to find adoptive homes for recovering animals, then let them know not only how much money was gained, but how many prospective homes for dogs were located. You might say something like this:

> Thanks to your generous sponsorship, the Third Annual Adopt a Friend Community Outreach was a phenomenal success. Over 500 people visited the event and we were able to place 45 of these wonderful, neglected dogs in loving homes. The activity also raised public awareness of the plight of these abused animals, and $20,000 was raised to continue the work of the Golden Retriever Rescue Center. This would not have been possible without your compassion and willingness to partner with us in the worthy mission.

An announcement like the one above thanks your sponsor, tells them how many people saw their signs and received the gift bags with their promotional items in one day. It also lets them know that this was an extremely effective venue for them to invest in. The sponsor who supported this obviously shares your concern about neglected animals, and you have made them realize that, through your organization, they have become active participants in a solution to the problem. You have not just touted what your organization has done; you have made them a partner with you and emphasized the value of their ongoing sponsorship. Make certain to take pictures of the animals interacting with families and children at the event as well. Who wouldn't love a picture of a beautiful retriever licking the face of a five-year-old child?

It is very important that you let the sponsors know what they have gained. If your event was a 5K fundraiser, let them know not only how many runners participated, but also how many people watched the race. If the local restaurant owner knows that 3,500 people in the neighborhood surrounding his establishment saw his advertising at the event he will be more likely to recognize the great advertising value this is for him and will be prepared to continue in a sponsor relationship with your organization and possibly increase his support in future years.

So what about the sponsors who are not involved in a big publicized event? These are the sponsors that underwrite the cost of your website, provide hot lunch on Wednesdays for your inner-city day care center, pay the Internet service bill for the tutoring center, and a myriad of other day-to-day activities. It's easy to sell the package, thank the sponsor and detail the benefits he will receive—then don't forget to continue building that relationship.

Just like in a marriage, it is easy to take someone for granted when they are with you every day. It is important to schedule regular times to connect with these sponsors and to find ways to help them to continue reaping a benefit. Make certain the relationship not only remains mutually beneficial, but that the sponsor is updated on the favorable exposure he is receiving.

How to Create Continuous Value For Sponsors:

- **Give the sponsors advertised on your website updates on the number of visitors to your site.** It doesn't help, though, if you are not doing anything to increase those numbers. Some ways to increase awareness of your site is to create a blog and leave comments on other blogs related to your type of service with back links to your site. Include the web address in all correspondence. Post video clips of fun activities or events and then advertise the clips in the newsletter.

- **Maintain a newsletter and mailing list.** Periodically include a small feature on one of these faithful sponsors. State what they do in their own business, how they assist your organization and the great benefit you derive.

- **Pictures.** If they provide a service that is directly used by your clientele, include pictures in the sponsor spotlight showing your clients eating the free lunch or working in the computer lab.

- **When you have an activity you plan to spotlight in a local community paper, take pictures that show any sponsor plaques, signs or banners in the background.** If these are published, mail a copy of the article with a personal note to the sponsor, and provide a link to a scanned version on the website.

THE THANK YOU

> *"There is no such thing as gratitude unexpressed. If it is unexpressed, it is plain old-fashioned ingratitude."*
>
> — *Robert Brault*

Saying thank you is extremely obvious, but it is often overlooked. Foundation managers complain that many of the organizations to whom they have awarded grants and sponsorships fail to even say "thank you." This is inexcusable. Don't let your organization receive the call asking if a sponsor's check was received because you have been too busy to acknowledge the gift promptly.

Here are some rules you can follow to make certain that your organization never lets this important matter fall through the cracks:

- **SAY THANK YOU THREE TIMES IN THREE DIFFERENT WAYS.** Acknowledge the gift when it is first received with a personalized thank you letter. Send an update after the event, once more expressing your appreciation for their partnership. Acknowledge the sponsor's contribution in your newsletter and make certain a copy is sent to the sponsor. List the sponsors of your event in the press release. Send a thank you card signed by some of your clientele that have benefited from the gift. Be creative; there are a lot of ways to show gratitude.

- **MAKE THE THANK YOU A PRIORITY.** Assign the task to a specific person and then have a protocol of recording on the sponsor's record what has been sent, when, and by whom. If a phone call was made, write down who received the call and a brief summary of what was said.

- **HAVE SOMEONE ASSIGNED TO MAKE CERTAIN THE CONTACTS HAVE BEEN MADE.** Be accountable to one another. Sometimes ingratitude is inadvertent. Relieved that the event has been a success, the staff will naturally turn their attention to the next task at hand and could possibly forget about the sponsors who made the event a success.

- **THINK LONG TERM.** If you view a sponsor as a one-hit funder, then forgetting to express gratitude is easier. If you are looking for long-term partnerships you will naturally continue to cultivate the relationships.

- **BE SINCERE.** Don't overstate your case. Just as everyone can tell the difference between a compliment and false flattery, your sponsor will know if you are over the top in your comments. This is part of maintaining the trust. For example, if you want to thank the company that provided water for your runners at the 5k event, don't tell them that they alone were responsible for the success of the event and the entire organization would have fallen apart without their contribution—especially if 20 other sponsors took part.

FOLLOW UP

Many of the steps involved in providing good follow up have already been covered in previous sections, but it is important to step back and look at the complete scope of sponsorship. You need to do more than follow up with the sponsors you have already recruited. What about the prospects who did not respond with a commitment after your first or second visit? While you need to take care of your current sponsors, a vibrant, growing organization must always be pursuing new partnerships. This way your organization will not have to curtail the services it provides if a sponsor goes out of business or changes its funding focus. New sources of income also enable your group to continue to grow and expand its outreach to a larger community.

Make certain that these prospects receive your newsletter. This is helpful in so many ways. First, they have the opportunity to get to know you. They will see your work in action and after several months will come to realize that your organization has stability and permanence.

Next, they will see who else is sponsoring your group because of the spotlights you include on sponsored events and activities and on the individual sponsors as well. This serves the same purpose that references serve for applicants and contractors seeking jobs. Seeing that other organizations believe in you and support you will make your prospects more likely to trust you with their sponsorship as well.

Finally, they will get an opportunity to see the value you provide for your sponsors when they read the sponsor spotlights in the newsletter. After all, it could be their organization getting that kind of publicity.

Assign someone to continue making periodic contacts with prospects. Vary the approach and respect their time, but don't just write off prospects who don't sign on immediately. You are building relationships, and these take time to mature and ripen.

Follow-up also extends to your vendors, media contacts and any local businesses that allowed you to post a promotional flyer in the window or at their counter. Stop back in to those locations to remove the flyer after the event, drop off a thank you note for their assistance and give an update about the success of the event. This will make them more willing to assist you in the future. Who knows, in time that contact may become a sponsor for some need you have in the future.

Send thank you notes to your caterers. Let them know that they did a great job and you will be happy to refer them to other organizations. It can be easy to forget to foster these relationships—that is, until you want to try to get a discounted price for your next order. Vendors are much more likely to hear complaints when things go wrong, but absolutely nothing when things go right. Reverse the trend; they will remember you for it.

Most of all, follow-up and thanks go to your team. Have you ever worked on a team that was successful in not only reaching a goal or milestone, but surpassing it, and then there was no thanks? If so, how did that make you feel? Remember that your team of board members, volunteers, production crew, etc. are all vital parts of your team. Be sure to thank all of these people in a way that is meaningful to them. If you are looking great book on acknowledging others then I recommend *Blazing A TRAIL To Success: The New Art and Science of Acknowledgment* by Scott Degraffenreid.

At this point you now have a foundation on the sponsorship process and ways that you could partner with organizations and corporations to help create the service organization of your dreams. As discussed earlier in the book, sponsors are looking for long-term relationships and to create multi-year agreements with your organization. They perfect time to do this is 2-3 weeks after your successful event and once you've already thanked them (at least twice) for their support of the event, your organization and the community.

In fundraising it is easier to maintain a sustaining donor than to recruit new donors and the same applies to the sponsorship world. It is far easier to renew a sponsorship agreement than securing it for the very first time.

HERE ARE THE KEYS TO YOUR SUCCESS IN RENEWALS:

- Start early in the process. Start to pitch renewals within 45 days of the completion of the first event they sponsored.

- Ask your sponsor what they liked most about the partnership.

- Ask them what improvements could be made.

- Ask them if they are interested in renewing and when you can meet to discuss.

- Pretend they are a new sponsor, and start your research back at square one.

- NEVER offer the same exact sponsorship package. You can have similar levels, but the benefits and pricing should not be the same unless they are signing a multi-year deal.

While most sponsors will be happy to renew on an annual or multi-year basis, do not be offended should a sponsor not renew. There are several business reasons why a sponsor might not be able to renew, with the number one reason being budget cuts. Be sure to ask why they are not renewing, and ask if there is anything you could do to be a better fit for their organization in the future.

If they are not renewing due to missed milestones, ask to work with them to create a plan to resolve the problem and then follow that plan. Also, be sure to ask if you can contact them in the future for possible sponsorship opportunities, once you have rectified the current situation. Above all, be respectful and remember that a non-renewal isn't meant to be personal. You might even ask them if they know someone that would be a better fit for your organization and ask for the introduction. Continue to thank the organization for their support to date and keep them in the loop with other successes that your organization has.

Sometimes people fear asking for support because they feel guilty making the request. They are afraid that a sponsorship might present an unwanted burden for the prospect, but this is actually not the case. Foundations and many corporations have a requirement within their bylaws and in their annual budgets to contribute a certain amount of money or a percentage of profits to charitable organizations within the community.

They are literally looking for organizations that meet their funding guidelines. You should approach your sponsorship campaign with the knowledge that you are actually helping these prospects to find the best use for those allotted funds. And why shouldn't some of that support go to your organization?

GETTING THE MOST FROM THIS BOOK

Reading this book is a great first step to building a vibrant sponsorship program for your organization. You can refer back to it as a user manual, but it will not build your sponsorship base for you; only you can do that and now is the time to start.

If you are new to the entire sponsorship concept, start small. Target an event, activity or certain daily operational expenses that could benefit from a sponsor. Use this guide to put together a package and proposal, create a list of prospects, and then go have fun. Yes, that's right, have fun. You are going out to meet the people who will become friends and partners of your organization for years to come. It takes time and persistence, but the rewards are far greater than the effort.

GLOSSARY

Here is a glossary of terms that will assist you in your sponsorship process. Although some of these terms are not discussed in this book, the terms provided are commonly used by most corporations offering corporate sponsorships.

ACTIVATION: Any marketing, public relations or other activities a company implements to promote a new sponsorship. All costs associated with activation are in addition to the fee paid for the sponsorship.

ADDED VALUE: An extra benefit given to a sponsor or prospect. Mainly used to close a deal, offer more value, or to build stronger relationships.

AGENT: The individual representative or organization that solicits sponsorships on a commission basis.

BRAND LOYALTY: The act of customers consistently re-purchasing the items or services from a store or provider. Several factors affect this loyalty including: values, price, quality, branding, and customer service.

CROSS PROMOTION: When two or more organizations or individuals partner to create marketing and public relations efforts that benefit all parties involved.

DEMOGRAPHICS: Information used to provide a clear picture of the target market for your sponsored property. This information can include age, gender, income, occupation, or any other information gathered for research purposes.

DONATION: Any product, service, or gift that is given to an organization without measurable results or contractual obligations.

EXCLUSIVITY: The exclusive rights of sponsorship, ad sales, or exhibit booths. Exclusivity is generally a right purchased by business category for the event or sponsored property.

IN-KIND SPONSORSHIP: Full or partial payment for a sponsorship offered through products, services, or other non-cash methods. This is commonly known as contra or trade.

MARKETING MESSAGE: The message a sponsor wants to share through their sponsorship. Marketing messages can be around the launch of a new product, a set of shared values, or any other message important to the sponsor at the time of the campaign. Be sure the marketing message of your sponsor matches your core values.

NICHE MARKETING: Marketing focused at a specific group of individuals within a set target market. (e.g.: Lifetime: Television for Women)

OFFICIAL SUPPLIER/VENDOR: This is often a low cost sponsorship in which a supplier and/or vendor pays a sponsorship fee to guarantee that they will receive a certain amount of business or rights to sell at the event. (e.g.: The Official Car, The Official Beverage, etc.)

POINT OF DIFFERENCE: The key event details and sponsor benefits that set an event or organization apart from competitive events.

REPORTING: Providing updates to sponsors regarding the event and specific milestones that have been met.

SIGNAGE: Signs displayed at an event that feature the logo or marketing message of a sponsor.

SPONSEE: The individual or organization receiving sponsorship funds from the sponsor.

SPONSOR: The individual or organization that purchases the sponsorship property offered by the sponsee.

SPONSORSHIP PLAN: A document that details how a sponsorship will be serviced by the sponsee.

Resources

What follows are resources and tools to help you in developing and executing your Sponsorship Campaigns.

Please know that the companies and resources listed below are ones that I've used in the past or have been referred to and the information is current as of the publication date of this book; however, you need to pick the service provider that works best for your organization! I am not responsible for the outcome of any business decision you make, nor for any company that you hire as a result of my recommendation.

My intention is to make it easier for you to know who to work with, but you MUST do your own due diligence to make the best decision for your organization. I have not accepted any fees or any other sponsorship and/or consideration from any resources listed.

(cont. on next page)

ASSOCIATIONS

AMERICAN MARKETING ASSOCIATION *(MarketingPower.com)*

The American Marketing Association (AMA) is the professional association for individuals and organizations who are leading the practice, teaching, and development of marketing worldwide.

ATTORNEYS

OPTIMA LAW GROUP, APC *(OptimaLawGroup.net)*

(Non-profit / Corporate Formation, Contracts & Agreements)

Tom Jurgensen
9990 Mesa Rim Road, Suite 250
San Diego, CA 92121
http://www.optimalawgroup.net/

RESEARCH

HOOVER'S ONLINE *(Hoovers.com)*

IEG *(Sponsorship.com)*

PROSPECT RESEARCH ONLINE *(iwave.com)*

Prospect Research Online (PRO) is the leading online database created solely for non profit organizations to assist in their fundraising research.

Prospect Research Online provides detailed information on individuals, foundations and corporations—information that is invaluable for your organization when sourcing major gifts. Prospect Research Online includes all of PRO's Tools PLUS the following data providers and/or their database for your use.

Tax Planning and Accounting

Cohesive Tax *(CohesiveTax.com)*

Karla Dennis, CEO & Enrolled Agent
1 (800) 878-4051

COHESIVE is a professional tax and accounting firm employing distinguished tax professionals specializing in complex tax situations, tax preparation and resolving tax issues.

The firm prides itself as a complete taxation and book-keeping service to individuals and businesses, serving the community, region and national clients for nearly two decades. COHESIVE offers unsurpassed expertise in the field of accounting and taxation including preparing tax returns, representing clients in audits and collections issues that may come before the Internal Revenue Service.

You have a clean slate every day you wake up. You have a chance every single morning to make that change and be the person you want to be. You just have to decide to do it. Decide today's the day. Say it, 'this is going to be my day.'

— BRENDON BURCHARD

ABOUT THE AUTHOR

ABOUT ROBERTO

Roberto C. Candelaria, creator of the definitive fundraising guide, *Cash for Your Cause: How to Raise Five Figures in 30 Days* and author of *Relationships Raise Money: A Guide to Corporate Sponsorship*, is President of Calidad Marketing LLC, a boutique consulting firm helping for-profit and non-profit organizations across the globe accomplish their mission. A long-time non-profit veteran, Roberto has learned the non-profit and corporate sponsorship world from the ground up.

After seeing first hand the impact a well-run organization can have on the community, Roberto dedicated his life to teaching organizations profitability, growth, and long-term sustainability. An inspiring leader and in-demand speaker, trainer and coach, Roberto has helped hundreds of leaders and organizations more effectively raise funds and execute their mission. As one client recently said, "If you follow his plan, success is inevitable." Roberto's products and presentations on: sponsorship, board development & governance, corporate sponsorships, online fundraising and event planning & management, have made him an in-demand, innovative expert. For more information, please visit:

HumanReturns.com

RelationshipsRaiseMoney.com

SponsorshipBootCamp.com

Roberto can be reached at:

877-991-9925

Info@HumanReturns.com

Coaching Programs

Looking for a deeper dive into securing corporate sponsorships? Now is time for your organization to climb out of the money pit and into the sponsorship cloud with our new Sponsorship Boot Camp program.

Beginning in December 2011, Roberto and his team will begin offering a home study coaching program, Sponsorship Boot Camp, based on *Relationships Raise Money: A Guide to Corporate Sponsorship*.

Acquiring funding for your organization (for-profit or non-profit) can be as simple as knowing the difference between asking for money and proving a viable funding opportunity. This self paced coaching program will dive more deeply into the sponsorship process with coaching modules that include sample pitches and proposals that my team has used to secure sponsorship funding from organizations such as BMW, DELL, Southwest Airlines, and State Farm Insurance—to name a few.

LEARN MORE ABOUT SPONSORSHIP BOOT CAMP ONLINE AT

SPONSORSHIPBOOTCAMP.COM

...WAIT, THERE'S MORE!

For over ten years, Roberto has energized audiences across America, educating organizations about the power of appreciating human returns and building sustainable relationships. Non-profits are all about giving, and your time is a precious commodity. Learn how to maximize your output by focusing on the organization's most valuable resource: its people.

Roberto learned first-hand how sustainable relationships form the foundation of every thriving organization. He is a unique trainer, who inspires his audiences with fresh ideas by merging new thoughts with a familiar framework, thus enabling real and rapid learning.

Invite Roberto and his team to serve your organization through:

- Corporate Training Programs
- Live Seminars
- Keynote Speaking
- Customized Coaching Packages

FOR MORE INFORMATION, PLEASE VISIT:

HUMANRETURNS.COM

INFO@HUMANRETURNS.COM | 877-991-9925

READY TO JUMPSTART YOUR FUNDRAISING?

CASH FOR YOUR CAUSE WILL GIVE YOU THE SYSTEM TO:

- ✓ Expand the personal relationships of your organization...
- ✓ Find fundraising challenging and rewarding...
- ✓ Launch an effective, inexpensive grassroots campaign that provides a great return on investment...
- ✓ Harness the power of social media...
- ✓ Establish positive fundraising habits that can be used over time...
- ✓ Put out the best possible effort in order to earn donations for your organization...

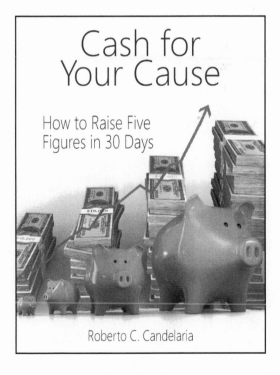

ORDER YOUR COPY TODAY AT HUMANRETURNS.COM